McINDOE'S ARMY

McIndoe's Army

THE STORY OF THE
GUINEA PIG CLUB AND
ITS INDOMITABLE MEMBERS

EDWARD BISHOP

GRUB STREET · LONDON

Published by
Grub Street
The Basement
10 Chivalry Road
London SW11 1HT

British Library Cataloguing in Publication Data
Bishop, Edward, 1924-
    McIndoe's army, the story of the Guinea Pig Club and its
    indomitable members. – New ed.
    1. Guinea Pig Club – History. 2. Surgery, Plastic – England –
    London – History. 3. Surgery, Military – England – London – History.
    I. Title. II. The Guinea Pig Club.
    617.9'9'0592

ISBN 1 902304 93 4

Typeset by Pearl Graphics, Hemel Hempstead

Printed and bound in Great Britain by
Biddles Ltd, Guildford and King's Lynn

Author's Note
Quotations heading each chapter are taken from the
speeches and writings of the late Sir Archibald McIndoe
unless otherwise attributed.

CONTENTS

ACKNOWLEDGEMENTS

This story contains some very personal information for the use of which I am indebted to the committee of the Guinea Pig Club, members of the club collectively and many individual guinea pigs, some of whom have died since my first encounters with the club in the early 1960s.

Much of the information was volunteered verbally, or was provided in writing by individual guinea pigs. *Guinea Pig*, the club magazine, has been an especially fruitful source of material, as was access to post-war Guinea Pig Club correspondence.

I am indebted to Lady McIndoe and her stepdaughter Vanora Marland, each of whom have helped in so many ways since we first met some forty years ago. Nor, as readers will become aware, would this account of the Guinea Pig Club have been possible but for the assistance, advice, and encouragement over the years of the late Group Captain Tom Gleave, the late Dr Russell Davies and the late Edward 'Blackie' Blacksell.

More recently, James 'Sandy' Sandeman-Allen, Jack Allaway, Jack Toper, Dr Tom Cochrane and Bill Simpson have been similarly helpful, as again will be apparent. I am particularly indebted to Bill Simpson for his kind permission to use material from *The Way of Recovery* and *I Burned My Fingers*. I am also indebted to Robert Marchant, curator of the Guinea Pig Museum at the Queen Victoria Hospital, for assisting me at the museum, and providing some of the illustrations and for his historical guidance.

Finally, I thank John Davies for welcoming me to Grub Street's list and Louise King for whose painstaking yet painless editing I am also indebted.

THE GUINEA PIG ANTHEM

We are McIndoe's army
We are his Guinea Pigs.
With dermatomes and pedicles,
Glass eyes, false teeth and wigs.
And when we get our discharge
We'll shout with all our might:
'Per ardua ad astra,'
We'd rather drink than fight.

John Hunter runs the gas works,
Ross Tilley wields a knife.
And if they are not careful
They'll have your flaming life.
So, Guinea Pigs, stand steady
For all your surgeons' calls
And if their hands aren't steady
They'll whip off both your ears.

We've had some mad Australians,
Some French, some Czechs, some Poles.
We've even had some Yankees,
God bless their precious souls.
While as for the Canadians
Ah! That's a different thing.
They couldn't stand our accent
And built a separate Wing.

We are McIndoe's army, *(As first verse.)*

FOREWORD

By the late SIR ARCHIBALD H. McINDOE
in a message to the magazine *Guinea Pig*, April, 1948.

One day someone will tell the complete story of Ward III[1] in the way it should be told. Richard Hillary, Tom Gleave and Bill Simpson have told their personal experiences and their own stories, but there is a wider field than the purely personal one. The future writer will tell of the return of the men of Dunkirk, tired but undismayed, who found their first rest there; of the Battle of Britain fought overhead, and the burned pilots who came to regard the place as home, gave it its particular flavour and then went back to fight carrying a card inscribed "in case of further trouble deliver the bits to Ward III, East Grinstead" . . .

Throughout the ups and downs of the war . . . Ward III sat more or less in the front line, a hive of activity, always busy, never dull.

He will tell of the Guinea Pig Club, how and why it started, what it achieved and what has become of all the Guinea Pigs who did not go down to defeat but rose from defeat to victory. Perhaps too, of the vast gifts which came from America, Canada, Australia, South Africa and New Zealand, and recognise the sacrifice of those who went back to fight and who encountered The Last Enemy . . . .

Had there been no Ward III there would not be today the great hospital which is making a real contribution to international understanding and friendship . . . .

This is the story to be told before the name that was Ward III sinks into oblivion. It is a great story and worthy of the telling.

---

[1] Throughout the book, the author has followed the more common usage, Ward 3, except where McIndoe refers to it as Ward III in his writings.

PROLOGUE

"We do well to remember that the privilege of dying for one's country is not equal to the privilege of living for it."

The valediction to his guinea pigs of Sir Archibald McIndoe.

In the course of research for my book *The Battle of Britain* which was published in 1960 for the twentieth anniversary of the Battle I encountered Group Captain Tom Gleave who had been shot down in flames and burnt while commanding No 253, a Hurricane squadron.

Tom explained his scarred appearance and new nose and urged me to follow *The Battle of Britain* with a book telling the story of the Guinea Pig Club so far as it was then known.

He told me he was the chief guinea pig and invited me to my first 'lost weekend' which with good reason guinea pigs have always known the club's annual reunion and dinner.

I knew instinctively I had found my next subject and noted my first impressions:

"Some wear dinner-jackets. Some wear suits. Some look prosperous and are. Some look prosperous and are not. None look as badly off as some are. But an odd-man-out at their dinner, a whole, unscathed man, will recall such appearances later.

"Here at table, one of the long finger tables leading from the knuckle table where sit the chief guinea pig, the controller of the RAF Benevolent Fund, the chief philanthropists, the chief surgeons, the chief physicians, it is the sight of the hands which mesmerises the uninitiated. Stumps, knuckles, contracted claws. Hands that have been roasted raw, red and tissued . . . .

"The odd man, bearing the legs, arms, hands, fingers, eyes and hair, nose and ears with which he was born, shifts his legs gingerly in the knowledge that under the table there are injured feet in heavy surgical boots, and government legs which are taken off every night, complete with shoes and socks.

"Then, carrying enough Dutch courage to meet his hosts eye to eye (or eye to glass or plastic eye) the guest at the annual dinner of the Guinea Pig Club learns that talk releases a personality from behind each mask of facial plastic surgery. Meeting the men within he forgets the scars, the flaccid grafted skin, the wigs, the immobile masks which here and there bizarrely resemble the painted expression of a circus clown. He remembers that the outward appearance of the men at table may be the legacy of less than one minute in a burning, exploding, crashing war plane and of many years in and out of the Queen Victoria Hospital at East Grinstead."

Some forty years afterwards when so many who attended that dinner are dead I flinch at the insensitivity of my description, but I let it stand as matter of record. When I attended this year's (2001) 60th anniversary dinners, the first in February to accommodate the busy diary of HRH Prince Philip, Duke of Edinburgh, the president of the Guinea Pig Club, and the second in September as is the annual tradition, I marvelled at members' management of the additional infirmities of age.

Familiarity with the disfigurement of burns and maxiliofacial injuries and the individual styles of eating and drinking which a lifetime of practice has perfected had long since banished uneasiness. Rather my thoughts turned to the toll time has taken of guinea pigs who survived the 1939-45 war.

It was not, of course, announced but the Guinea Pig Club estimates that of the 649 guinea pigs who survived and made new lives – often in unimaginable adverse circumstances – only some 144 remain, of whom 97 are resident in Britain and the remainder in the Commonwealth, continental Europe and elsewhere in the world.

In recent years an additional and final toast has appeared on the reunion dinner menu. At the February dinner the president, members and guests raised their glasses and drank 'To The Last Guinea Pig'.

Edward Bishop
St. Leonard's-on-Sea, 2001

CHAPTER ONE

"The development of this unique organisation from a meeting of the 'Few' in 1941 round a bottle of sherry to its present flourishing condition is one of the curiosities of the war."

Tom Gleave, who was the chief guinea pig until he died in 1994 asked: "Will you write a book about the Guinea Pig Club? Not about Archie McIndoe. But the book *he* always wanted. The story of his guinea pigs, the men he re-made and who, as he often reminded people, helped to make him." Tom's face, hands, arms and legs were burned in the Battle of Britain. "Standard Hurricane burns", Tom called them after a German cannon shell had hit the fuel tank of his fighter in 1940.

Archie McIndoe gave Tom a new nose and there was a large patch of pale, dead-looking skin on Tom's forehead because that was where his nose came from. The patch looked lifeless because it had replaced the skin of the nose Tom had been born with and was foreign to his face. It had come from his thigh.

The new nose was the major job in Tom Gleave's facial repair. It settled down as a large, healthy looking nose and because the skin of one's nose and of one's forehead is very much of the same texture it tended to flush obligingly after a pint or two of best bitter; or for that matter of 'ordinary'. Tom's skin, like the rankless society of the Guinea Pig Club, accepted no draught bitter distinctions.

Towards the end of 1940, Tom began his "tour of ops" at the Queen Victoria Hospital, East Grinstead, but he was not yet known as a guinea pig or a member of 'McIndoe's Army'. McIndoe's patients began to call themselves guinea

1

pigs at Christmas and the Guinea Pig Club was not founded until the following summer.

Surgically, the growing of Tom's new nose is known as a rhinoplasty. Archie McIndoe curled the skin from the squadron leader's forehead and grew it where the fire in the Hurricane cockpit had so consumed his nose that it had shriveled his nostrils into two tiny holes by his eyes.

Tom said: "At the beginning of the war it was thought that the best thing to do with badly injured airmen was to tuck them away quietly in a country institution where they would never be seen again and would be spared having to face the world. It seemed kinder to protect us from the public gaze and it was also believed that the sight of chaps like us would depress the public and with them the general war morale."

Tom's half-moon spectacles slid to the tip of the nose that Archie McIndoe had grown and sculptured for him. The fire in his Hurricane had caught his eyelashes and burned away the eyelids which had saved his eyes. Watering, friendly, tired eyes. Tired, perhaps, by the wartime Whitehall papers which Tom read as an official war historian after leaving the Service. Like the majority of McIndoe's Army, Tom was in the post-war years – as he always put it – "up to his new eyelids in work".

He was not hidden away out of sight and out of mind as might so easily have happened had not the combined efforts of McIndoe, his team at the Queen Victoria Hospital, and the caring and supportive people of East Grinstead averted the threat of such grievously disabled, disfigured and mutilated men being institutionalised.

* * *

The Guinea Pig Club was born of the Sunday morning hangover which most of Ward 3 at the East Grinstead hospital had earned on the night of July 19th, 1941. "Let's have a grogging party", somebody said. Those who could move shuffled to a hut next door where the surgeons kept a 'mess' and Frankie Truhlar, a Czech fighter pilot, uncorked a bottle of sherry. There would have been other willing barmen had they had hands capable of the task. Frankie, who was the only patient in a sufficiently advanced state of repair, played host.

The clouds above East Grinstead parted to unration the sun, but Ward 3 was not a large airy ward like the windowed wards in the main buildings of this modern cottage hospital. The RAF burns patients were accommodated in a little brown wooden former Army hut at the back of the main hospital. Officially, McIndoe's operating theatre and Ward 3 were designated a Maxilio-Facial Unit.

It was long a popular misconception that Sir Archibald McIndoe, 'the Boss' or 'the Maestro' as his guinea pigs affectionately knew him, brilliantly conceived the idea of the Guinea Pig Club. This was not so. When the sherry had submerged the hangovers on that Sunday morning in 1941 the heavily bandaged fliers decided that the grogging parties were such fun that they would form a grogging club. A meeting was called and minutes were headed: "The Maxillonian Club whose members call themselves guinea pigs."

Pilot Officer Geoffrey Page, who, after being repaired and resuming combat, was to return to the hospital as a squadron leader with further wounds, took the minutes. He wrote:

"The objects of the Club are to promote good fellowship among, and to maintain contact with, approved frequenters of Queen Victoria Cottage Hospital.

There are three classes of membership, all having equal rights:

1. The Guinea Pigs (patients).

2. The Scientists (doctors, surgeons and members of the medical staff).

3. The Royal Society for Prevention of Cruelty to Guinea Pigs. (Those friends and benefactors who by their interest in the hospital and patients make the life of the Guinea Pig a happy one.)

The annual subscription for all members is 2s/6d, due on the 1st July each year. Women are not eligible for membership, but a 'ladies' evening may be held at the direction of the Committee.

The following members were proposed and seconded by members present.

President: Mr A. H. McIndoe, F.R.C.S.

Vice President: Squadron Leader T. Gleave

Secretary: F/O. W. Towers-Perkins

Treasurer: P/O. P. C. Weeks

Committee members: Messrs. Coote, Edmonds, Page, Hughes, Wilton, Overeijnder, Gardiner, Russell Davies, Fraser, Hunter, Eckoff, Morley and Livingstone.

Other members present were: Messrs McLeod, Mappin, Clarkson and Bodenham.

The following were proposed and seconded as members: Messrs Dewar, Shephard, Lock, Hillary, Fleming, Lord, Hart, Langdale, Bennions, Harrison, Butcher, Truhlar, Koukal, Noble, Mann, Krasnodebski, McPhail, Banham and Smith-Barry."

At the time none of the men in the hutted ward's black iron beds could have foreseen where their Sunday grogging party would lead them and the movement they had started. Nor could McIndoe or Gleave have imagined the serious burden their titles of president and vice-president, light-hearted as they appeared in the context of a grogging club, were to lay upon them for so long as they lived. Nor, that following the death of Archie McIndoe in 1960 his successor as president would be HRH Prince Philip, Duke of Edinburgh who, serving at sea in the Royal Navy in wartime, had been as junior as many of the guinea pigs themselves.

That at the outset the club's founders looked little further than an excuse for grogging and a vehicle for raising spirits in Ward 3 was demonstrated by the light-hearted reasons advanced in Geoff Page's minutes for the respective appointments of Bill Towers-Perkins and Peter Weeks as secretary and treasurer respectively. The former was picked because, physically, he could not write and the latter because, being unable to walk, he could not make off with the funds.

In the glow of the sherry the Maxillonians showed perception. Peter prepared the ground for future treasurers who were to raise large sums to help to support guinea pigs in need and in later years to make handsome donations to the RAF Benevolent Fund, for long an ever ready supporter of individual guinea pigs as need arose.

If by the same inverted criteria Geoff Page, the twenty-one-year-old Battle of Britain fighter pilot who took the minutes, was perhaps the least clerically inclined of this gallant company, his guinea pig credentials were impeccable. Refusing to be dissuaded by his uncle Sir Frederick Handley Page, the pioneer aircraft manufacturer, that pilots were two a penny, Geoff had learned to fly with the air squadron while studying engineering at London University.

Sensitive and imaginative, serving in No 56, a Hawker Hurricane squadron, Geoff had destroyed three enemy bombers in mid-July, 1940, when he noted in a letter: "It fascinates me beyond belief to see my bullets striking home and then to see the Hun breaking up before me. It also makes me feel sick. Where are we going and how will it all end? I need someone to talk to me who isn't tied up in this legalised murder."

As the battle wore on fatigue slowed Geoff's reactions and the stress of frequent sorties frayed his nerves. On August 17 he had been scrambled to intercept "a gaggle of Dornier bombers" off the Kent coast when "drowning in fear, fatigue and nervous exhaustion", he was shot down over Epple Bay and baled out of a blazing cockpit.

Water rather than fire brought Derek Martin to the Queen Victoria Hospital as one of McIndoe's earliest guinea pigs. When the grogging party took place he was in Kindersley, a ward in the main hospital, but he was very soon enrolled. Derek was the twenty-year-old skipper of a giant four-engine Short Sunderland flying boat, at the time the largest operational aircraft in the world, when on the afternoon of March 14, 1941, he was ordered from Oban on the Argyll coast in Scotland to search for a U-boat suspected in waters south of Iceland.

In the early hours of the following morning and after an uneventful twelve-hour sortie landing conditions at Oban were abysmal. Mist denied Derek an opportunity to estimate his height above the sea which in any event was too calm to provide him with a datum to assist his judgement above the water. In the circumstances he crashed and the next thing he knew he was under water.

Derek blessed the silence and wondered whether he was dead until somehow, free of the wreckage, he came to the surface and floated in the icy sea. He was hoisted aboard a rescue boat and placed on his back. Someone said: "This one's dead" and threw a blanket over him. On the way to the West Highland Hospital at Oban Derek's wings and buttons were removed and he was relieved of his wallet and gold watch.

At the hospital doctors resuscitated the 'dead' pilot and stitched up as much as possible of his scalp and face. Visiting fellow flying-boat pilots confirmed that at first Derek had been written off and told him his left eye had been hanging out of its torn socket and his scalp attached by only an inch of skin. He also discovered that six members of his crew had died and others were seriously injured.

It was an inauspicious beginning to Derek's war but thanks to McIndoe's skills he resumed operational flying in war and peace. When in 1973, (following a second near fatal accident serving in 1970 with Nato in Norway) Derek was finally invalided out he had served as a wartime chief of staff in the Cocos Islands, commanded a Meteor jet fighter station and specialised in electronics intelligence. In a busy 'retirement' he was to serve his fellow guinea pigs as a committee member. He was particularly able in providing advice on war pensions. Outside club matters he found time for a range of activities including co-founding the RAF Gliding and Soaring Association and undertaking various acts of public service among which serving on the committee of Sport for the Disabled.

While considering the roll call of the club's founder members note the name Bennions minuted by Geoff Page between Langdale and Harrison. In Battle of Britain terms the experience of George Bennions differed little in general from the majority of his fellows excepting perhaps that he was a former Halton apprentice who had been recommended for a cadetship at the RAF College, Cranwell, and become a fighter pilot. After being wounded by a shell splinter in his left heel he had remained operational and shot down four Me 109s in rapid succession.

Many years afterwards when the RAF's Battle of Britain Memorial Flight, still a great and emotive attraction at nationwide airshows, agreed to allow its AB 910 Spitfire to be associated with a Spitfire flown by a guinea pig, it adopted EB:J. These were the letters carried by George Bennions's No 41 Squadron aircraft the day he was shot down, losing his left eye and suffering other wounds, one of which left his brain exposed. On the same day his DFC was gazetted.

This splendid gesture became doubly warranted when it was discovered that Eric Lock, another founder member, also flew with No 41 Squadron. Son of a Shropshire farmer Eric was a twenty-year-old Spitfire pilot when on September 5, 1940, he destroyed three Me 109s and was awarded the DFC. After reaching a total of fifteen in October he was awarded a Bar.

On November 17 Eric had shot down two Me 109s over the Thames estuary when he was jumped by a Me 109 and severely wounded in his right arm and both legs. In December 1940, while being treated at the Queen Victoria Hospital, he was awarded the DSO. The next year and already a fully-fledged guinea pig Eric resumed operational flying. On August 3, piloting a No 611 Squadron Spitfire adorned with twenty-six swastikas representing his high score he spotted German troops on a road near Calais and dived to strafe them. He was never seen again. He is remembered on the Runnymede Memorial.

Jack Fleming, who was also a Battle of Britain fighter

pilot, partly owed his good fortune in being transferred from an RAF hospital to the 'Sty' – the guinea pigs' name for the Queen Victoria – to McIndoe's soft spot for New Zealanders. Jack had been awarded a permanent commission in 1939 and was flying a Hurricane with No 605 (County of Warwick) Auxiliary Air Force Squadron when on September 8, 1940, he was shot down in flames over Tunbridge Wells in Kent.

After turning the blazing fighter on its back twice Fleming, a heavy rugby player, managed on the third attempt to heave himself out, taking the cockpit hood on his shoulders. For whatever reason his parachute failed to open until he had dropped 20,000 feet. He was taken to nearby Wrotham Cottage Hospital and put to bed among twelve expectant mothers before being removed to RAF Halton where, temporarily blinded with burned eyeballs, he refused to have both legs amputated at the hip.

Jack had been given up as a hopeless case when Archie McIndoe, making one of his periodical trawls of RAF hospitals, arranged his transfer to the Queen Victoria where saline baths, which were still experimental, were highly effective. Although he did not fly operationally again, Jack remained in the Service until 1959. After retiring as a wing commander he was a member of the club committee for many years.

There must have been many wartime drinking sessions among the Services at which the most solemn of pledges were taken to meet regularly and to remain a band of brothers. A club. Some of these great intentions died with the next day's hangover. Others lingered and disappeared with the last shillings of a gratuity. Few survived.

It is doubtful if the guinea pigs could have been born in hospital conditions other than those which the club's founders, encouraged by McIndoe, helped to create for themselves at East Grinstead; *encouraged by McIndoe* because a grogging club was far outside the normal routine of hospitals, civil or Service, even in wartime.

Ward 3 itself was peculiarly conducive to the development of a club atmosphere. To the exclusivity of accommodating very badly burned airmen the ward added the mystique of being just a nondescript wooden hut. As a gang of smugglers might have remembered their deepest cave, so in their own way the guinea pigs drew inspiration from the hut which became the shrine of their Sty and the spirit of guinea piggery. The birth of this spirit was aided, of course, by Ward 3's accommodation of men wounded in two of the most stirring episodes of British history, the Dunkirk evacuation and the Battle of Britain.

There were of course pilots burned earlier in flying accidents, as with Harold 'Birdy' Bird-Wilson who went on to become a Battle of Britain ace. Shortly after the outbreak of war in 1939 Birdy was piloting a BA Swallow light civil aircraft when it crashed in bad weather. He was fortunate to survive the accident in which his passenger, a fellow RAF officer, was killed, and he was badly burned. Although Birdy's plastic surgery at the Queen Victoria Hospital preceded the formation of the Guinea Pig Club he was later invited to join.

McIndoe completed Birdy's new nose in time for him to resume with No 17, a Hurricane squadron and fight with distinction in the fall of France during May and June 1940, and in the Battle of Britain until he was shot down over the Thames estuary by Adolf Galland, the German ace. Birdy was burned again when his cockpit caught fire. He baled out and was picked up by a motor torpedo boat.

Although shrapnel from the guns of Galland's Me 109 was still embedded in his body he went on to destroy a total of six enemy aircraft. Birdy retained vivid memories of attacking formations of more than 100 aircraft as he piloted one of a mere twelve Hurricanes. He recalled: "Your throat dried up as you got nearer. I don't believe any man who said he wasn't afraid." Birdy became a successful fighter leader and was awarded a DSO, DFC and Bar and AFC. He retired in 1974 as an air vice-marshal.

Incidentally, Birdy was one of at least three Battle of Britain pilots understood to have become guinea pigs under the guns of Adolf Galland. Others included Pat Wells and Jackie Mann (who many years afterwards was to achieve a somewhat different notoriety as a Beirut hostage). Pat Wells recalled: "I was hacked down in a Hurricane over Kent and was well fried. I was taken to an emergency hospital at Leeds Castle and some days later transferred to Ward 3 at East Grinstead.

"I must admit that initially I thought I had been admitted to a lunatic asylum, the noise was unbelievable with radio music blaring, patients shouting above the noise in conversation. In due course I became like the rest of them." Subsequent research indicated that Pilot Officer Wells had been shot down by Galland, who then sent him a copy of a combat report in which he had listed him as kill No 56. In 1995 Galland invited Pat to Germany and they became firm friends.

Some guinea pigs, as with Birdy whose family circumstances had rendered him responsible for himself since boyhood, were self-reliant and felt no need of subsequent support, but the majority were blessed by McIndoe's mantle. In mid-war when guinea pigs had burst the plank walls of Ward 3 and spread into the new and more conventional (only in the architectural sense) wards which the Canadians and Americans added to the hospital, Archie McIndoe cited specific pigs as *his* reason for starting the Guinea Pig Club. He never intended to take the credit for creating the club.

Yet he never passed up an opportunity, with a little white lying if necessary, to present a very badly injured pig as his reason for nurturing it if he thought this would strengthen the member's case for a higher disability pension or a particular peacetime job. Among so many reasons this was an important factor in McIndoe's claim: "The development of this unique organisation from a meeting of the 'Few' in 1941 round a bottle of sherry is one of the curiosities of the war."

The Guinea Pig Club was as brilliantly unplanned as any of Britain's best success stories! Certainly no official mind could have decreed:

"We'll put the burned airmen in an uncomfortable wooden hut at the back of the Queen Victoria Cottage Hospital. There they will create an amazing spirit, bringing to it the spirit of the fighter squadrons.

"Then, when we get more and more burned airmen from the heavy bombers – among some of whom the morale may not be so high because they will not necessarily be the cream like these chaps – the spirit will have wafted through the hospital and everybody will get better much quicker as a result of our ingenious plan. Some may even return to the war and use again the killing skills which it has cost the nation so much time and money to teach them.

"Meanwhile, just to help the chaps along we'll recruit the prettiest nurses we can find for this very special hospital and we'll put a fellow called McIndoe in charge of the lot because he seems not only pretty capable at carving people up but also in understanding their minds – and it is every bit as important to understand people as to graft their skin when dealing with burns cases.

"Oh yes, one more very important point. We should find a hospital where the matron will be a thoroughly good sort, smile sweetly and take Mr McIndoe in her stride. She must welcome beer barrels in the wards and will not have to mind when some of her patients return from the London night-clubs in time for breakfast.The cottage hospital of East Grinstead then, is entirely suitable. Matron Hall is a gem and has a talent for turning a blind eye.

"Ah, another point. Anaesthesia for plastic surgery is a specialised branch of medicine and like Mr McIndoe the anaethetists must be humanitarians. Team up Dr John Hunter and Dr Russell Davies. Finally, East Grinstead is a good healthy spot. Fresh clean Sussex air. Not too far from the night spots of London so that we can keep the chaps cheered up. There are also the scented pinewoods around. Mr McIndoe says they contain healing properties, better still for guinea pigs, they enclose the homes of some of the nation's wealthiest people. McIndoe enjoys the social life and he's just the man to persuade the rich to do the chaps well once they're on their crutches. A club? That's a top priority!"

Such perception would have been too much to expect of the official British mind.

So who was Archibald McIndoe, the surgeon who was so providentially in the right place at the right time and how did his arrival at East Grinstead coincide with the development of a cosy cottage hospital into the Queen

Victoria Hospital which under his leadership and inspiration became the centre of excellence, especially in plastic surgery, which it remains to this day?

In the mid-1930s the little hospital which had been founded in the prevailing spirit of nineteenth century Victorian philanthropy was earmarked by a government emergency services committee for treatment of maxilio-facial injuries in the event of war.

Legend has it that the decision was strongly influenced by Sir Harold Gillies, the pioneer First World War plastic surgeon who as a Royal Army Medical Corps (RAMC) captain had set up a unit with 200 beds at Aldershot. Conveniently, East Grinstead was on the route between his home and his golf club at Rye in East Sussex. Geographically, East Grinstead also suited Sir Kelsey Fry, the distinguished oral surgeon, whose son attended the nearby Brambletye preparatory school.

The government bought additional land on which to build hutted wards to accommodate 100 people. Thus, when war came on September 3, 1939, McIndoe was already installed as hospital director. Soon thereafter he was appointed consultant in plastic surgery to the RAF.

McIndoe was thirty-nine and owed his initial recognition to Gillies who was a distant cousin and fellow New Zealander. After studying at New Zealand's Otago medical school and taking up a fellowship at the Mayo Clinic in the United States, McIndoe, introduced by Gillies, became clinical assistant in plastic surgery at St Bartholomew's Hospital (Barts), London.

He went on to develop his surgery skills as plastic surgeon to Barts, Chelsea Hospital, the Hampstead Children's Hospital, the Croydon General Hospital and elsewhere. Thus, as McIndoe arrived at East Grinstead he was already one of Britain's leading surgeons in his field.

* * *

"Throughout the ups and downs of the war . . . Ward III sat more or less in the front line . . ." McIndoe reminded guinea pigs in his message to the first number of their magazine. Agreed, but the hospital at Orpington to which Tom Gleave's 'fried' body was delivered when he was shot down defending London was even more in the front line during the Battle of Britain than the Queen Victoria at East Grinstead.

Tom had been leading an attack on a formation of Ju 88 bombers when his Hurricane caught fire. He recalled:

> "A long spout of flame was issuing from the hollow starboard wing-root, curling up along the port side of the cockpit and then across towards my right shoulder. I had some crazy notion that if I rocked the aircraft and skidded, losing speed, the fire might go out. Not a bit of it. The flames increased until the cockpit was like the centre of a blow-lamp nozzle. There was nothing left to do but bale out. A forced landing was out of the question as I was still 7,000 to 8,000 feet up. I reached down to pull the radio telephone lead out of its socket but the heat was too great. The skin was already rising off my right wrist and hand and my left hand was starting to blister, the glove being already partially burnt off. My shoes and slacks must have been burning all this time but I cannot remember any great pain."

Squadron Leader Gleave undid his cockpit harness and tried to raise himself. Finding he was too weak he was prepared to shoot himself if he could not escape. He always flew with a loaded revolver. He pulled off his helmet, though this was not without a struggle, and opened the cockpit cover. He had decided to roll the Hurricane on to her back and to hope to fall out but before he could do so there was a great flash and his burning body was thrown clear. Tom was burning and turning over and over in the air, yet with no sense of falling. He found the rip-cord handle and it was only later that he realised that the fire and his escape had happened in less than a minute. A pilot had little chance of surviving more than a minute in a blazing Hurricane.

* * *

When the sirens sounded patients at Orpington were placed under their beds. The first time Tom recovered consciousness after an emergency operation, he found himself under a bed. "There's a battle going on overhead", said Blossom his nurse.That night his night nurse told him: "We have several RAF pilots in the hospital as well as many Dunkirk casualties." The siren sounded again as she was speaking and Tom was lifted out of bed and back into his 'shelter' under its mattress and springs which was the best they could do for him. The floor shook as the anti-aircraft guns opened up and Tom could hear the whistle of bombs. A nurse knelt beside him. When the bombs were falling she put one hand on his shoulder and the other on the cage protecting his burned legs and sprawled protectively across him.

Tom remembered:

> "There was a terrific crump. Then another and another. The building seemed repeatedly to leave the ground and come back, thud, thud, thud. Then came a lull. I asked for a drink and some ice. My mouth was parched and the corners of it seemed to tear apart as I tried to speak. Nurse brought a bowl of ice cubes and a glass of iced water. Then she placed some ice in my mouth, repeating this every ten minutes. It was delicious.
>
> "Again we heard the drone of the Hun and then the bombs came crashing down around us. It went on for hours and all the time my nurse crouched beside me, placing more ice in my mouth and adjusting my pillow from time to time."

She gave Tom a sleeping draught. Such a badly injured man could have too much of the front line.

Tom Gleave continued:

> "One afternoon – it may have been the next day – I was awake. Sister said that my wife had arrived. I was well enough to worry about Beryl seeing me as I was. My hands, forehead and legs were encased in dried tannic acid. My face, which felt the size of the proverbial melon, was treated in the same way and I peered through slits in the mask.
>
> "I heard footsteps approaching the bed and then saw my wife standing gazing at me. She flushed a little and said, 'What on earth have you been doing with

yourself, darling?' 'Had a row with a German', I replied. She tried to smile and sat down by my side. It was not until I saw my face in a mirror weeks later that I realised how brave she had been."

Like many of his fellow 'fried' pigs, Tom Gleave, the chief guinea pig, passed several weeks in a delirium. "A world, half real, half fanciful", he said. "I can remember some times when Blossom would bend over me and I would find something different about her. For it would be Beryl."

One night when the nurses had lowered Tom into his air-raid shelter he thought he was in a room where the ceiling was very low and people were walking about ducking their heads. "I became involved in a heated argument and a fight, people were trying to hold me down but I lashed out, sometimes burying my hands in the ceiling and bringing plaster down on the floor."

Emerging from the delirium, Tom found his night nurse exhausted and that the tannic acid on his hands had flaked away in the course of his battle with her and the bed-springs overhead. Tom's delirious period was easing when he was told that a new treatment for burns, which did not involve tannic acid, was being given at a special unit at East Grinstead and he was to be transferred to that hospital because it also specialised in skin grafting and plastic surgery.

When Archie McIndoe examined Tom's face at East Grinstead he told him: "We can do either of two things with that nose of yours. We can graft a piece of skin on to it and give it some sort of covering. Or, we can give you a new nose. This latter method will be quite a big job but well worth it." Tom opted for a new nose.

It was not until his first leave from the hospital that he became conscious of the effect of his disfigured appearance upon other people and even then, feeling very much the same man inside, it seemed to him at first that people were staring at "a fellow wearing a great-coat that was now two or three sizes too big for him and a collar that showed a wide gap all round." He was helped, he said, by the maestro's observation: "They can get used to it and *like* it!"

In the middle of repair Tom was told that he looked a more terrifying sight than he would when all his plastic surgery had been completed and he found courage to confront himself, thinking: "Go on, have a good look. I won't be like this much longer." In any event, another matter was worrying him very much more than the horror or compassion of strangers in the street.

He was a regular officer and had commanded a fighter squadron yet he had temporarily lost his sense of self-respect, a loss which owed nothing to his disfigurement. "It rankled to have been shot down", he said. "I was touchy about being out of the war and this was not conducive to an even temper – but Beryl took it all in her stride. Only once did I come near to lifting the lid off the pot. I was doing some short-range shopping for Beryl which took me to a little bread shop. I shuffled in and asked for a loaf. The lady behind the counter took one look at my face and quickly forgot my order. 'And what have you been doing sonny?' she asked. 'I had a spot of bother up there', I said, pointing upwards. 'Oh well', she said, 'I suppose you did your best.'"

* * *

Some of the names which were among those in the minutes of the grogging club will be familiar, notably that of Richard Hillary, whose book *The Last Enemy* in which he tells of Ward 3, is a classic of war literature. But only those knowledgeable about the First World War, who can recognise the tie of the Royal Flying Corps and can recall the Gosport system of flying instruction will remember the double-barrelled name of Lieutenant Colonel Smith-Barry who introduced it.

Among those listed as founder members of the Guinea Pig Club Robert Smith-Barry, who had dropped several ranks to return to the Service as a fifty-four-year-old pilot officer ferry pilot, had crashed a Blenheim bomber during the Battle of Britain and broken his jaw.

McIndoe had been very doubtful about the propriety of sparing a bed for Smith-Barry. Yet had he known the future benefits of friendship with this veteran airman to the welfare of his guinea pigs he would – with his customary oppor-tunism – have assured him not only a bed but also a red carpet all the way from the ambulance which delivered him.

As it was, the surgeon felt that he had been bounced into accepting him after taking a telephone call from the wealthy Colonel Phillipi who had flown with Smith-Barry in the Great War. "Mr McIndoe? Good. Now look here. I want you to provide a private room, a beautiful nurse, a vi-sprung mattress and your personal attention four times a day for a friend called Smith-Barry. He's already been in two hospitals and had himself removed because he doesn't like being messed about. Now he wants to come to East Grinstead."

Smith-Barry had heard of Ward 3's reputation as a remarkable haven where patients were treated as individuals and he was determined to take advantage of this relaxed regime. No sooner had he been received than he entered wholeheartedly into the spirit of guinea piggery and he was the first of a number of airmen who were to organise, in the wartime meaning of the word, an 'escape' from the rigours of ordinary hospitals and achieve admittance at the Queen Victoria Cottage Hospital – the Sty.

In later years, it amused Archie McIndoe, employing his effulgent, after-a-good-dinner technique, to recall the manner of Smith-Barry's arrival:

"If I remember, I was fairly hostile to the whole idea and even more so when a spanking great ambulance arrived complete with two obvious old hands from World War I, of whom I had never heard.

"Such, however, was the charm of manner of George Phillipi that my irritation was rapidly allayed, the private room and nurse were produced, the soft bed supplied and I found myself visiting Robert Smith-Barry more than four times a day.

"One day Smith-Barry came to me and said that his ancient carcass could be of little use to the air force and could I and would I use it as a source of skin for the young men under my care. As gently as possible I told him there was only one Smith-Barry and that his skin was no use, but that if he really wanted to help me, he could come to East Grinstead and act as a sort of liaison officer between Air Ministry and E.G. Promptly he said that in the field of negotiation he was no good at all but that his friend George Phillipi was superb at it and he would persuade him to come."

The Guinea Pig Club, in embryo, persuaded the air force of the need for an office at the Air Ministry to care for its welfare problems and very soon a department established for the purpose and named P.5 appeared at Adastral House. To run it, Colonel George Phillipi was freshly commissioned as a distinctly venerable pilot officer. With Pilot Officer Phillipi looking after the pigs' interests at the Air Ministry and elsewhere, it was necessary for him to talk day-to-day detail with somebody other than McIndoe at East Grinstead. He found 'Blackie'.

CHAPTER TWO

"Blackie was a natural in the field of human relationships and is today, in my opinion, one of the really great experts in the business."

'Blackie' was the guinea pigs' affectionate name for Edward Blacksell, for many post-war years headmaster of the Barnstaple Secondary Modern School, a director of the English Stage Company (The Royal Court Theatre) and the large, shaggy dogsbody to the Guinea Pig Club, which he became sixty years ago when, supplied by Phillipi, he arrived at Ward 3 with his PT kit.

Smith-Barry's chivalrous, if unrealistic, offer of his own skin, had brought Phillipi into guinea piggery and Phillipi had sent for the man whom he had been told could persuade young airmen to believe in PT – a discipline which any veteran who once upon a time volunteered to fight Germany and Japan will remember as seeming merely time-wasting to young men tearing their hearts out to win their wings and get into the war.

Thus a baffled Blackie, an assistant schoolmaster from North Devon who had done no serious PT before joining the RAF, found himself posted to the Queen Victoria Hospital, East Grinstead.

Blackie had hoped to join the Royal Navy and it was only when the doctors rejected him that he volunteered for the RAF where he was recommended for training in that muscular world of ropes, weights and wall bars, the School for Physical Training Instructors.

His selection for this course came about in a curious fashion, although it never appeared odd to guinea pigs who were to discover how fate habitually tilted their beloved Blackie at life. Blackie had reported to the former airship base of Cardington. There, standing tall, thin and with that anxious, slightly stooping, angle of attention of most tall recruits until it has been drilled out of them, he was interviewed by the type of resurrected officer who, as with Smith-Barry, would have been one classed as a 'dug out'. The dug out, charged with allocating an RAF trade to the young school-teacher with an English degree, gazed out of his office window and at that moment saw a party of men marching a great distance away. He beckoned Blackie outside. "Shout at those men", he ordered. "If you can persuade them to double over here, I've got a job for you."

If there was one talent which might serve Blackie well in the air force, it was his ability to make himself heard – and obeyed. Bleak winter afternoons spent playing football at Barnstaple had acclimatised his lungs to doing battle with the wind from Exmoor. The dug out's airmen doubled over, thus asssuring Blackie's future as a physical training instructor and, inadvertently, a great future for the Guinea Pig Club.

Early in his new career Blackie was posted to Plymouth in Devon where the high-spirited Australians of the Royal Australian Air Force's No 10 Squadron equipped with Sunderland flying-boats were deemed to require taming. He devised an assault course, described by the Aussies as a "real bastard" and promised to provide a barrel of beer when each and every man had beaten his time to complete it. The challenge appealed to the Australians. No sooner had they been tamed and the barrel consumed than a puzzled Sergeant Blacksell was ordered to report to Mr Archibald McIndoe, at the Queen Victoria Hospital, East Grinstead.

"Good God", exclaimed a legless and horrified guinea pig when Blackie laid out his gym shoes, shorts and PT instructor's vest on a bed in Ward 3, "you're not doing PT with us!" But the guinea pigs to their delight very soon discovered that the sergeant was no knees-bend, arms-upward-stretch automaton. He enjoyed beer and, as significantly, for their future benefit he gave promise of contributing forcefully to alleviating the hostilities which had already opened under the McIndoe umbrella between them and the Service and civil authorities.

One of the first battles took place shortly after Blackie's arrival. Guinea pigs remember it as 'The Battle of the Blues' because it arose from the issue of government hospital blue uniforms and red ties and an order to wear them. The airmen were proud of their air force uniforms and hard earned flying brevets. They feared that clad in shapeless blues they might be mistaken for prisoners in some penal battalion or special class of convict. Henry Standen, citing the white shirt, orange-red tie and blue uniform, commented: "We were glad to fight for the flag but not to parade East Grinstead in it."

The boss agreed with his guinea pigs that the hospital blues of 1914-18 were as out of date as hospitals without barrels of beer in the wards and as the bureaucratic insistence on describing military patients as 'invalids', leaving the impression that they were permanent cripples. The guinea pigs collected the hospital blue uniforms and burned them on a bonfire and he gave his blessing to their initiative coupled with the warning: "For heaven's sake don't spoil the blackout." The surgeon did not want his aircrew repair shop blown to bits by enemy bomber crews.

The bonfire may have escaped the notice of the German raiders but its smoke, like the coiling smoke signals of Red Indians of Western films, did not escape a nosey and interfering guardian of good order, discipline and red tape.

An Air Ministry staff officer accompanied by a posse of RAF red caps descended upon the the disfigured wrecks of burned and mutilated airmen, who hobbled about the hostelries of East Grinstead in RAF uniforms or any assortment of clothing they could muster rather than appear in the detested hospital blues.

The strutting arrival of the belted and gaitered RAF military police with short haircuts and highly polished chins caused much amusement among the 'mutinous' guinea pigs who had been so smashed up in His Majesty's service. Yet they tempered their outward mirth with serious gratitude for McIndoe's decision never to accept the rank of air vice-marshal which he had been offered. Remaining a civilian surgeon at a civilian hospital, although he had been appointed consultant in plastic surgery to the RAF, he was well placed to repel such attacks.

As George Taylor, an Australian guinea pig, remembered, the maestro "reflected his usual craftiness by preventing the authorities from bringing their plans to fruition." Archie McIndoe discovered the Air Ministry had authorised all ranks to dress in sports clothes when on the way to take part in sport. Consequently, he arranged that all tennis courts, squash courts and a swimming pool in the neighbourhood of East Grinstead should be open to his patients.

The red caps were stymied, confronted as they were by the spectacle of disfigured men, heavily bandaged men, men on crutches, in wheelchairs, men helping each other along like participants in a three-legged race and declaring: "on our way to tennis and squash and to swimming." The RAF military police turned about and were not seen again. In any event, apart from the depressing influence they bore on the guinea pigs' morale, hospital blues were impractical dress for many of them. Stiff government flybuttons were difficult to adjust. Old, well-worn grey flannels were much handier, especially when guinea pig comfort was later much enhanced by a stock of zips sent over from Canada.

There was also the important consideration of the maintenance of the guinea pigs' rankless society. Air Ministry insistence upon blues for men below the rank of warrant officer but freedom for those more senior, was regarded as contrary to the club's belief, developed from McIndoe's opinion that a badly burned man was a badly burned man irrespective of whether he was an air marshal or an aircraftman second class.

Although McIndoe always conceded that less freedom and more discipline would have provided better therapy for some of his guinea pigs, he reckoned that such cases numbered only some two per cent of the total and he did not intend to allow the Air Ministry to make ninety-eight per cent of his patients suffer for such a small minority.

The majority of aircrew officers readily accepted the irrelevance of rank in the Guinea Pig Club. Not least Bill Simpson, a pre-war short service commission officer who welcomed the relaxation of rank barriers. But for the severity of his condition and rapidity of the German advance during the fall of France in May 1940, Bill, "fried and mashed", in his own description, might have joined

Tom Gleave, Geoff Page and other early guinea pigs at the grogging party.

As it was, Bill was piloting an obsolescent Fairey Battle single-engine light bomber in a suicidal treetop attack by No 12 Squadron at the outset of Germany's May 10, 1940 *blitzkrieg* (lightning war) invasion of the Low Countries when ground fire ripped a hole in the Battle's engine. As his bombs hit a column of advancing troops and attendant mule train, lumps of molten metal streaked back from the stricken engine and fumes filled the cockpit.

He remembered: "Great sheets of searing flame rushed between my legs and up to thirty feet above me. In that first rush of heat my hands were burned and they seized up solid." He was enveloped in fire and paralysed by fear and slumped "in horrified resignation and waited for death." Crazily, the aircraft's screaming klaxon continued to remind him to lower his wheels before landing.

Bill was on fire when he was dragged clear of the wreckage by his observer and air-gunner who rolled him in the damp grass while the Battle exploded and burned and exploded again. What horrified him most was the sight of his hands. "They were the hands of a ghost – bone white. The skin hung from them like long icicles. The fingers were burned and pointed like the claws of a great white bird, distorted, pointed at the end like talons, ghastly thin." Bill asked himself: "What will I do now? What use will these paralysed talons be to me for the rest of my life if I *do* live?"

Later, as Bill lay for many months in a succession of French hospitals he wondered how Hope, his wife of a few months, would handle the horror of his hands and face. He was to note: "I was aware that Hope would be deeply shocked and in particular terribly upset about my hands. She had always taken great delight in them. They had been small, neat and immaculately manicured." Eventually, the enemy accepted that Bill could pose no possible future threat and sanctioned his repatriation, enabling him to return home in the autumn of 1941 via Spain and Portugal and put his fears about Hope to the test.

Unhappily, she had been inadequately prepared to receive her husband who, travel weary and clad in odd pieces of foreign clothing, scarred, eyes streaming, dirtily bandaged, smelly and clumsily disabled, met her in

Somerset at a Weston-Super-Mare hotel. He wrote: "All the horror she had always suffered at the sight of blood and mutilation spread through her being like a fever and she broke down and wept." Bill found it "bitterly ironical" that Hope's instinctive compassion hardened him against her. He knew "that no matter how gallantly she tried there was no way back." He was admitted to Ward 3, began prolonged surgery and encountered Blackie, who as with so many of Bill's fellow guinea pigs, was to help him along the hazardous route to an endurable and fulfilling life.

* * *

If Blackie possessed any ties other than the tie of the Guinea Pig Club with its distinctive RAF colours and winged Guinea Pig motif then they must have been little used. Blackie without his Guinea Pig Club tie would have seemed as naked as Gus Fowler, the guinea pig who joined a nudist colony.

Few unscathed men are privileged to wear the tie, though Blackie's tie was not entirely unearned by bed-hours and plastic surgery. The necessity for which was not, as jocularly alleged, due to his PT classes for East Grinstead nurses – the only PT guinea pigs countenanced at the Sty. Nor was it the result of the rag in which he was debagged and savaged by convalescent pigs at Marchwood Park.

Blackie's lengthy hospital treatment and plastic surgery had resulted from a serious motor accident in the 1950s. Over the years the fact that he failed to become a patient at the Queen Victoria Hospital invoked much mirth at the annual lost weekend. As the boss told guinea pigs shortly after the accident: "Blackie is lucky to be alive. He had a very unpleasant car accident and almost bought it. He is now really one of you. He had quite a bit of plastic surgery and I must say, they've done a darned good job on him, even though he did go to a rival firm."

The rival firm was the Oldstock Hospital at Salisbury. Blackie was wearing his club tie when an ambulance delivered him to the hospital where his guinea pig status assured his reception as a medical celebrity in every respect barring a red carpet, which the Oldstock did not possess.

Such was the reputation of the Queen Victoria Hospital's war record and the Ward 3 spirit that Blackie recalled: "Mention of EG and guinea pigs produced a respectful handling of the injured parts, a sweeping away of regulations . . ." Matron making her first ward round after Blackie's admission, stopped at his bed and observed to a sister that something was missing. "This man", matron said, "is a guinea pig. He needs a pint of beer."

Not long after Blackie recovered from his own plastic surgery he began to help a guinea pig whose situation serves well to introduce a theme which runs through all the actions of the Guinea Pig Club – readiness to provide relief of distress and repeated reassurance to members long, long after the end of their service life.

In 1942, at the start of his career as a guinea pig, Alan Morgan, a young industrial apprentice from Manchester who had volunteered for aircrew, had lain for days at East Grinstead in a very shocked and dazed condition. He was little aware of what was happening to him except that he knew that the nurses insisted upon keeping his hands immersed in buckets of ice. He could not appreciate that the doctors were trying to save his hands so that he could return to his trade after the war.

Blackie recalled that Alan's sole contribution to any attempt at conversation was: "This is a bloody place and they're all bloody mad in here", but what nobody then knew were the circumstances in which all the fingers of young Alan Morgan, a flight engineer, had been turned into black sticks which had to be kept immersed in a pair of ice buckets.

His bomber was high over Leipzig when it was attacked heavily by flak and the enemy fire burst open a door in the side of the aircraft. Two of his fellow aircrew, attempting to close the door, had passed out through lack of oxygen. Alan pulled them back from the dangerous opening and plugged them into the oxygen supply to bring them round. Then Alan lost consciousness and, as at that moment the bomber was attacked by fighters, no one could pull him away from the open door where he had fallen, his gloveless hands hanging out over Germany. Unlike most of his fellows in the ward whom he thought were "bloody mad", Alan was not fried but frost-bitten.

In time McIndoe and his team decided there was no chance of saving Alan's fingers and that his charcoal sticks were for the 'chop' as guinea pigs said. On the day he was listed for the operation Alan beseeched Blackie to stay with him in the theatre while they took his fingers off. Blackie not only watched the operation but he wheeled Alan in and out of the theatre. When Alan surfaced from the anaesthetic Blackie was at his bedside to explain what had happened. Rather than dwell on how much of his hand McIndoe had removed he emphasised that the surgeon had left part of each thumb and how much of a help this would be when Alan began to learn to use what remained to him. Then Blackie wrote, at Alan's dictation, to Ella, his girl in Manchester.

* * *

Possibly more difficult during wartime than reassuring the guinea pigs were Blackie's interviews with some of their friends and relations. Not all, as Ella was, were prepared to accept Blackie's sometimes somewhat overbearing manner. There was the day, for instance, when Jimmy Wright's father first encountered him on a visit to East Grinstead where Jimmy lay burned beyond recognition and blinded in both eyes, after the Marauder exploded in which he had been filming over Italy as a photographic reconnaissance cameraman.

In his job as an official war correspondent cameraman and newsreel executive, Mr Wright was accustomed to courteous attention from the highest ranking of officers wherever he went. Not the most temperate of men, he was already in a fairly aggressive mood when he arrived at the Queen Victoria Hospital to see his son. Indeed, he had been disturbed since the Army had informed him erroneously that his son had died in an Army hospital in Italy only to fly out and discover that a warrant officer had considered it administratively convenient to notify Jimmy's death in a comprehensive overnight casualty signal. The warrant officer had reckoned that no man who had been so badly burned could survive the night until morning.

Consequently, Jimmy's father recalled he "was very, very upset by the levity" with which Blackie, whom he described as "only a warrant officer", toyed with a squash racket when they first met and scrutinised him with such an air of authority that he might have been the chief of the air staff himself.

It is likely that but for his father's intervention the message that Jimmy had died on active service would very soon have been substantiated. Undoubtedly Mr Wright saved his son's life. With the help of a friendly American general he flew to Jimmy's side and found that he was being massively drugged. His experience of morphia while serving in the Royal Flying Corps on the western front and as a front-line cameraman in the Second World War told him that such doses would not only release Jimmy from pain but could also kill him. There was a dramatic moment at the hospital when standing at Jimmy's bedside he seized a syringe just as a nurse was about to administer the drug and dashed it to the floor.

Using his status as a war correspondent Mr Wright managed to arrange his son's repatriation. Fixing a flight home in a cargo Liberator he accompanied Jimmy as he lay bandaged from head to foot like a mummy and packed between two aero-engines. There were some frightening moments as the Liberator passed uncomfortably close to the heavily defended French Atlantic port of Brest until an escort of Spitfires arrived and Flying Officer Wright reached home in some style. His father was only later to learn about and appreciate the unorthodox spirit of guinea piggery. Meanwhile, cutting through red tape, he had saved his son, an airman the Army had declared dead, in the true spirit of the club of which Jimmy was to become one of the most popular members.

* * *

At his home on the Thames at Shepperton Jimmy talked about his RAF and guinea pig careers. He bought the house to be close to the film business he had built, a remarkable achievement for a blind man. There he had fended for himself since a manservant had taken advantage of his blindness and robbed him while he was in France, where the Guinea Pig Club had arranged special surgery in a final attempt to obtain some restoration of sight in one eye. So

Jimmy returned home to two disappointments. His man's disloyalty and a final realisation that there was no longer any hope that he would ever see again.

Like the matron who had admitted Blackie to hospital Jimmy insisted on a mug of beer, smiling: "You can't talk to a guinea pig without a pint." He poured out the beer and were it not for the glassy nothingness of his sky-blue eyes which, seeing nothing, were about all that remained of Jimmy's face, it would have appeared that he could see.

Generally, conversation with a totally or partially disfigured guinea pig requires communication through his eyes. A guinea pig's face will tell you little or nothing about his emotions. Plastic surgeons at the Queen Victoria could graft pieces of skin from donor areas elsewhere in the body but they could not replace the little muscles whose movements produced the smile that charmed, or on the darker side of character, the sneer or leer that might have occurred before fire destroyed a guinea pig's physical ability to produce facial expressions to match a mood.

Jimmy Wright's sightless eyes conveyed nothing. But his mouth was exquisitely contrived by the maestro and there was just enough movement to provide the smile which evidenced the quality in Jimmy Wright which Blackie described as "saintly". In Jimmy's medical file there was a photograph which showed Jimmy happy and smiling when he joined the RAF, an image of a good looking young man very pleased at being photographed for the first time in his new uniform.

This photograph guided McIndoe and his fellow plastic surgeons through the sixty operations they performed on him. Aided by the photograph and what remained of Jimmy Wright, they created a smile just like the one in the picture, the smile which brought Jimmy so many friends and grew the film business which he built. It was a smile which after a few moments of conversation, almost convinced one that he was not blind because one could so easily imagine his eyes lighting up as he visualised the television commercial or film documentary he was making or even the events of war which mutilated him.

Sixty years on from the founding of the Guinea Pig Club one needs reminding how much acceptance as aircrew in the RAF meant to young men like Jimmy Wright; how it enabled a new entry to tuck the white flash of aircrew under training into a forage cap and exit a class environment, high, low or middle and enter the honoured, privileged, glamourised company of men where the goal of a flying brevet and female adoration shaded the actuarial expectation of a very short life.

On his eighteenth birthday Jimmy Wright had volunteered for aircrew but he received a big disappointment when he was told his eyesight was not good enough. The disappointment was heightened because, his father having remained in the RAF for ten years after serving in the RFC during the First World War, Jimmy had grown up on RAF stations.

It has happened many times in war that a man who has failed to gain acceptance in an arm of the Services which demands supreme medical fitness has found himself more dangerously engaged than had he qualified medically in the first place. Jimmy Wright decided that as he could not train as a pilot he would take a civilian job until his call-up papers arrived. He joined the Technicolor film company, a move which was to lead to an RAF photographic course and a commission as an operational film cameraman; a hazardous occupation in which Jimmy could expect to lie in a bomber's nose and 'shoot' at low level in the face of concentrated enemy flak.

Before a member of the RAF Film Unit could join an operational squadron he was ordered to qualify in some respect as aircrew so that in an emergency he could leave his camera and fight. Thus Jimmy achieved his ambition to become aircrew. Qualifying as an air-gunner he sewed the single wing with the letters AG onto the tunic of his new pilot officer's uniform.

Pilot Officer Wright, air-gunner, reported to the Pinewood film studios where his part of the RAF unit was situated. He remembered that it seemed strange to be walking about the studios and film sets and taken for an actor playing a part. Sometimes he wondered whether he was real and if his smart new uniform had not been provided by the wardrobe department. As no-one of lesser rank troubled to salute he took the charitable view that *they* were the film extras.

Jimmy filmed his first bombing operations over France

and the Low Countries and was posted to the Desert Air
Force where he received a cool welcome. He recalled: "No.
223 Baltimore Squadron did not like the idea of having an
extra member joining their crews, however much he prided
himself as an air-gunner. This was because the Baltimore
was a small aircraft with very little room in which to move
about."

However, Jimmy settled in while also operating with the
Americans in Bostons and Mitchells during the Sicilian
campaign and the invasion of Italy. He experienced two
lucky escapes before the Marauder crash on take-off from
Taranto in which he was left for dead – until somebody
turned over his blackened body and said: "I think this
one's still alive, but he can't possibly live long."

In an earlier brush with death Jimmy had baled out of a
bomber shot down by anti-aircraft fire among the
mountains of central Italy. He very nearly went into the
mountains with the aircraft because he was not wearing his
parachute and had very little time to look round for a
harness. He found it as the bomber began to fall out of
control and landed just inside the Allied lines. He had been
lucky. In his haste he had put the harness on the wrong way
round, but had found the rip-cord side in time. Jimmy's
second escape took place when the American ship in which
he was returning to his new base headquarters at Naples
was hit by an aerial torpedo and he was rescued from
the sea.

When Jimmy Wright began surgery at East Grinstead, he
recognised the soft, confidence-giving voice of the
anaesthetist sending him to sleep in the operating theatre.
Many months earlier as a young assistant with Technicolor
Jimmy had filmed the wounds of a party of six guinea pigs
who had been conducted by a Dr Russell Davies to Sir
Harold Gillies' hospital at Basingstoke as subjects for an
instructional film.

He was not to know that before very long he would share
the plight of the six guinea pigs he had filmed and begin a
long association with Russell Davies who as medical
liaison officer of the Guinea Pig Club and consultant
anaesthetist to the Queen Victoria Hospital was one of the
best friends the guinea pigs ever had.

CHAPTER THREE

"Allied to Blackie's monumental labours . . . has been the work of Dr Russell Davies who has developed the uncanny capacity for handling pension cases."

On a wartime night when overhead the searchlight batteries between London and the coast were handing German raiders on from Sussex-by-the-Sea to the Serpentine, Dr Russell Davies could not get off to sleep at East Grinstead. Patients tend to presume a monopoly of insomnia but doctors can worry themselves into sleeplessness too. Even anaesthetists.

The worry which was keeping Russell Davies awake was derived not from his professional responsibilities for the guinea pigs as one of their anaesthetists but from his humanitarian concern for their future welfare. He was puzzled by the perplexing vagaries of the disability pensions which were beginning to be awarded. How, for example, had the official mind arrived at an award of ninety-two per cent for Henry Standen, grossly mutilated and with only the sight of half an eye remaining to him in a fearfully disfigured face? Why ninety-two per cent? Why the two per cent? Why not eighty-eight per cent or ninety-six per cent? Why had a pig who had lost *one* eye been awarded forty per cent while Jimmy Wright, sightless in both eyes, rated one hundred per cent? The questions kept Russell awake. He got out of bed, checked the blackout curtains, switched on a light, and began to write down his first thoughts on guinea pigs and pensions.

It was the beginning of a long quest and over the years the correspondence in his Guinea Pig Club filing cabinet built up a formidable collection of pension histories and bore witness to this persistent, methodical doctor's dogged spare-time pension advocacy on behalf of the guinea pigs. It was a self-imposed labour of love which, without fracturing his supremely conscientious professionalism, he could have permitted himself to forego.

Disturbed that sleepless night by the illogical nature of the government's early Second World War pension awards to Ward 3 patients, Russell Davies devoted the remaining hours to outlining a schedule designed to guide the award of disability pensions to burned people and other recipients of plastic surgery.

As he worked Russell visualised and valued many of the disabilities he had encountered at the hospital and assessed them in pounds, shillings and pence according to his own judgement. It was a long night's work, perhaps the best night's work that anyone concerned with the welfare of wounded service people has ever done. By morning Russell Davies had arrived at what he believed to be a fair and reasonable guide to the assessment of pension awards for some of the many permutations of disablement. Fairer, certainly, than the schedule of which a pensions official had told him conversationally: "Roughly speaking, we say fifty per cent for half an injured face and one hundred per cent for a whole injured face and start from there."

The pensions people had no scale for guinea pigs and it angered Russell Davies that the guinea pigs were suffering from rough-and-ready calculations. Accustomed to anaesthetising airmen on the operating table who were having new eyelids fashioned from the soft skin under their arms and at the same time losing a leg – just one example of the many permutations of guinea pig disablement – Russell Davies was determined to sell his belief that some were so badly injured that a maximum rating of one hundred per cent was not sufficient.

On that sleepless night, Russell Davies rated the worst cases at 170 per cent and worked from that basis, with the result that henceforth the Guinea Pig Club succeeded in obtaining the maximum of one hundred per cent for members who previously might have rated less than one hundred per cent, say, ninety-two per cent as in the case of Henry Standen.

The consequence of Russell's scale was that the club launched its long battle "to end", as Blackie characteristically insisted, "any such nonsense as any one-eyed member receiving less than a one hundred per cent disability pension."

No punches were pulled in this pensions battle. "To settle matters", Blackie remembered, "Archie took a top official to the Savage Club. 'Agree to our ratings', he said, 'or I'll send them back and back again to you and kick up hell in the House.'" On another occasion, McIndoe wrote to Blackie: "I have written to the ministry re the pensions and am arranging an interview so that we can stop this fantastic nonsense of giving Jock Morris fifty per cent pension and cutting Ross Stewart's pension down to seventy per cent. If they remain bloody-minded, you and Sir Ian Fraser can scare the political daylights out of the . . ."

The club's success in the pensions battle did not mean, however, that men as mutilated as Jimmy Wright received a 170 per cent disability pension. Authority always withstood McIndoe's pressure for the *official* acceptance of Russell Davies's scale, which included what the Guinea Pig Club terms, 'social disability'. But, the club was reassured that the pensions people were quietly relieved to resort to the guidance of Russell's ratings, supported from the outset by a verbal blitz in which McIndoe blasted Whitehall with salvoes of New Zealand invective and the dispatch of six trial guinea pigs to test authority's professed intention to improve the early pension awards.

Thenceforth, the disability pensions of members of the club were awarded with a more progressive attitude and following McIndoe and Russell Davies's first wartime offensive, and Russell's patient reasoning in case after case, created a pensions guide for guinea pigs. Indirectly, it also assisted less fortunate if equally badly wounded men from the Navy and the Army, who may not have been represented by such a strong lobby as the Guinea Pig Club.

The boss missed no opportunity of reminding guinea pigs of the potential 'trade union' power of their club. As the years passed, he increased the emphasis which he placed upon it in reunion dinner speeches and in 1956 he told the club: "Most of the guinea pigs are doing nicely, apart from such things as the credit squeeze and overdrafts

– although we do occasionally get the odd panic telephone call to say that the bums are in, please do something. The whole point is that you should stick together and no power on earth can hurt you. *Drift apart – and you've had it!"*

Appealing to his guinea pigs to help him to act on their fellow members' behalf and maintain the club's role of a union influence he pressed them to reach out a hand and drag any who strayed back to the fold "so that we may try to help them."

McIndoe was a master at keeping contact without necessarily seeing people. He toiled at the correspondence with which he kept in touch with his guinea pigs. Sometimes it took not a hand but a very long arm indeed to reach out to an East Grinstead patient as removed from the Sty as René Marchecourt on Rangiroa Island, Tahiti, in the French Society Islands. But the boss corresponded with René, who remained remembered, as he wrote from Tahiti: "Quite a lonely place. Just an atoll with a big lagoon in the middle where I am looking after my family coconuts."

* * *

The full measure of Russell's devotion to the guinea pigs was known only to the club committee and to those guinea pigs who were helped by him. It was always possible in the early years that at any time some members were not 'doing nicely' and needed assistance but were unaware of the help the club could give them, especially the effect a letter from McIndoe, Russell Davies or Edward Blacksell could have in certain quarters.

Sadly, following the maestro's death in 1960, neither the name on the letterhead nor the implied wrath of Sir Archibald McIndoe could be employed but when Prince Philip graciously accepted the presidency of the Guinea Pig Club, members were delighted. While, obviously, it would be improper to associate the Prince with any club business, guinea pigs have long been comforted that neither the Prince nor authority takes lightly any good cause with which he is associated.

Russell and his successors' continuing pressure to improve the disability pensions of certain pigs who have needed more help as they have grown older, was coupled with efforts to save others from the cuts which the nation, defaulting on its wartime debt, has attempted to impose from time to time.

Down the years since their pensions were so hard earned, the authorities have sought periodically to reduce some guinea pig disability pensions. Russell would receive a call: "I've been told to report for a pension board. What shall I say?" Russell invited the guinea pig to meet him and go through the papers. Where a cut seemed fair Russell advised acceptance. But if in his long experience Russell felt that the club should not countenance the cut then the old fight was on again.

One of the more callous instances of official inhumanity the club decided to combat began with a few words on an RAF notice-board. Without being vouchsafed so much as the privacy of a little buff envelope Michael E. Forster, who had flown Lancasters during the war, resumed with the RAFVR in 1949 and crashed three months later, read: "2606095 P.II Pilot Forster M. E. Discharged from the RAFVR on 1.3.50. Below the standard required for Air Force Service as a pilot."

Those last words bit into this badly burned pilot who had returned to the Service from civilian life. "It looked as though I might have been discharged because I couldn't make the grade as a pilot and not for medical reasons due to the crash", he told the club. "I am now in a bit of a state as I am trying to live on twenty-six shillings a week from National Health. What shall I do?"

In the accident Forster had sustained a compound fracture of the left ankle, a fractured left cheekbone, injury to the spine and multiple burns on face, neck, left arm, both hands, left leg, right knee and both feet. The club fought and obtained guinea pig Forster's one hundred per cent disability pension, with the relevant backdating.

Guinea pig Peter Brooke had been extensively burned, lost a hand and suffered multiple fractures, including a fracture of the spine. Few men could have been more distressingly injured and disfigured in the defence of his country. He was awarded a one hundred per cent disability pension. One would have supposed that the authorities would have been pleased to leave Peter's award at one hundred per cent for the remainder of his life, but not long after the award, they began to harry him with nasty little buff envelopes containing letters curtly informing him that his disability pension was being reduced by ten per cent. The club, wearing its trade union cap, went into action. Russell Davies prepared a pensions brief and McIndoe wrote to the Pensions Ministry: "This very gallant ex-member of aircrew received the most devastating injuries on May 8th, 1942, in action against Germany." Four months later, the battle won, the maestro was happy to write: "My dear Peter, I am delighted to hear that the ministry has repented and that all is well. If you have any further trouble with these gents, let me know."

Despite the uncanny capacity Russell Davies developed for dealing with 'these gents', it was understandable that there were many guinea pigs who may have been in need of his advice and were unaware of his continuing concern for their welfare – particularly the far-flung members of the club in Canada, Australia, and New Zealand.

It is natural to tend to remember old, but geographically distant friends as they were at the height of their association and fail to envisage them as they became. Thus, many surviving guinea pigs remember Russell Davies as they first knew him, a young doctor who had specialised in anaesthetics and who was not much older than most of them. They will remember him as a Celtically good-looking young Welsh doctor, and rather self-conscious in their company when they were in uniform and he was wearing a tweed jacket and grey flannel trousers.

They remember a young doctor who was really a craftsman in what they termed the 'knock-out-trade', but who was overshadowed by the bulky eminence of their great favourite, Dr John Hunter, the 'Pass Out King' – to whom, as they saw it, Russell compared as an able 'Pass Out apprentice'. This was an appraisal which physical comparison between John Hunter and Russell Davies confirmed. The two anaesthetists were men of contrast. John was 'The Giant Killer', full of joviality, blessed with a gargantuan public house thirst and a man who attracted nicknames. Russell was slight, diffident and deep.

John Hunter died before the boss. He had needed money to satisfy the demands of his expansive and generous personality and he made it in private practice as McIndoe's anaesthetist. He spent it as quickly as it came, much of it on parties for recuperating guinea pigs, vast rounds of drinks in the East Grinstead locals and ceaseless hospitality in support of a flow of well-told funny stories.

Often his drinking companions would be guinea pigs due, as they said, for the 'slab' and John Hunter's other anaesthetic the following day. For these guinea pig patients, the Pass Out King would frown upon spirits. Whisky, gin and rum as it was explained to them in lay terms, would send the blood through their veins faster than beer. So John tried to keep them on beer the night before a 'slabbing'. Jester to the Guinea Pig Club, John Hunter remained alive until the phase of drink and parties and the drowning of inhibitions had passed into the phase of job-finding, educational assistance, loans and grants and hard bargaining for pensions, for which Russell Davies was the more suitable advocate and mediator. When John Hunter died, a spray of cream carnations from the Guinea Pig Club lay on his coffin and a card bade farewell and carried a message which, recalled here, serves to perpetuate the true perspective of the relationship between the guinea pigs and their beloved Pass Out King: "In loving memory of and with great regret of Our John of the enormous heart from Guinea Pigs all over the world."

After John Hunter's death, Russell Davies refused McIndoe's invitation to join him as his anaesthetist in private practice, giving as his reason his principle that a doctor should work either privately or for the health service but not for both. But beyond this deeply felt principle there was another reason, though he never admitted to it publicly.

Russell felt strongly that while he remained full time at the Queen Victoria Hospital every guinea pig would be reassured that, despite the passing of time, there would be somebody always there, always at the Sty, who knew them and understood their eccentricities and their problems and was ready to fight for them whenever need arose.

But for this overriding sense of duty Russell Davies, while eschewing McIndoe's offer, would almost certainly have returned to a London teaching hospital. Indirectly, his decision to remain at the service of the Guinea Pig Club and its members assisted the cottage hospital to develop into the teaching hospital it has since become.

There are so many and varied examples of Russell's after-care and consideration that it is difficult to select from them. There is, however, one example which illustrates the delicacy of touch such advocacy can demand. It concerns Flying Officer Cyril Harper who crash-landed in the Malayan jungle after the war and subsequently, with the help of the club, qualified as an optician.

The most interesting aspect of Cyril Harper's story is that the main problem was not one which is generally taken into account when welfare and benevolent bodies survey a shattered serviceman's case. It was, however, by the very nature of the club's general rule that members should have served as aircrew, a problem which was common in the experience of the Guinea Pig Club. Simply, that Cyril Harper like so many young men who were commissioned as aircrew, had bettered himself through the opportunity which his Service career presented.

Ordinarily, had a whole, unbattered Harper returned to civilian life, it was possible that the initiative he had displayed in the RAF might have taken him ahead in a peacetime career. But, as a disabled guinea pig, he faced more than his fair share of hardship if he was to lift himself out of the railway station booking office, where he had been a junior clerk.

The helping of Harper required a finely balanced juggling of the resources from which the club could draw and here Russell played his part. He knew that, because the RAF Benevolent Fund was constituted to meet distress but never wholly to aid self-betterment, he could not seek complete assistance from that quarter for the financing of Harper while he studied for his British Optical Association Diploma.

He knew also that Harper had one cherished possession – a car. But he also knew that if Harper could show the sacrifice of parting with his car to help pay his way towards professional acceptance as an optician, such sacrifice would impress the RAF Benevolent Fund and the committee of the Guinea Pig Club.

Cyril Harper sold his car, although lack of transport hindered his mobility because his injuries prevented him walking comfortably or very far. Cash raised from the sale of his car provided one third of the sum he needed to see him through to a diploma – if he passed the exams. The Benevolent Fund contributed another third and the club made up the difference. Cyril Harper, former railway clerk, former flying officer, became an optician.

* * *

Mainly through his negotiations on behalf of Ian 'Jock' Craig who, true Scotsman, put his burns to work as a successful salesman of fire insurance, Russell Davies developed, in passing, a brilliant reputation among guinea pigs for negotiating the provision of glass eyes.

Jock Craig enjoyed telling the tale of his No. 9 glass eye but in common with all guinea pigs he preferred not to dwell on the fire which burned away the right side of his face. "We do not reminisce", Geoff Page reminded pigs at reunions and Blackie opined: "Reminiscence deeper than the schoolboy humour of the Sty recalls horror to some Pigs and is the negation of the euphoric world of guinea piggery into which Archie delivered them."

This much, however, Jock Craig was prepared to say and if it sounds matter-of-fact, then it is because it is the way he told the story:

> "Our bomber was returning to the station when it caught a wing in a balloon cable and plunged towards a bomb dump. I remember after the impact that I instinctively grabbed for my axe but it wasn't there. I made my way through the flames to the nose. Not a soul was there. No pilot. No front gunner. I worked aft again. The flames parted and I saw the ground. I jumped and then I ran and I ran and I ran, chased by rescuers. They caught me and tore my clothes off. I remember thinking that I had been No. 13 at my initial medical and No. 13 when I qualified. Then, as my tunic was ripped to pieces, I thought of my observer's wing on the breast pocket. 'Save that brevet', I shouted. 'It cost me four shillings.'"

Jock switched, by-passing the years in hospital, the many operations and talked about that glass eye. "Very disconcerting to find oneself on the point of selling some fire insurance and then out pops the glass eye, bounces off the client's desk and onto the floor. The trouble was that once having accepted a government glass eye, it was not easy to arrange to try out an alternative."

After considerable correspondence, Jock received seven possible substitute glass eyes on approval from the Ministry of Pensions. The canny Craig retained two, one to wear, one as a spare, never thinking that the extra eye would call for the advice and intervention of the Guinea Pig Club through the medium of its medical liaison officer, Russell Davies.

The ministry could not understand what practical use a one-glass-eyed man could possibly make of two government glass eyes. All Jock sought was the security of knowing that he carried a spare eye in his wallet.

At the conclusion of the correspondence and after more cost in time and postage than the price of the eye, which with his native sense of good husbandry he had retained, Jock Craig was allowed to keep the spare eye. But only after a special authority – "one No. 9 eye, Craig for the use of" – had been obtained from the Air Ministry.

* * *

The Guinea Pig Club, and in this connection for many years as represented by Russell Davies, was helped substantially in the peak years of presenting pension claims on behalf of members by individual guinea pigs' knowledge of their own medical and surgical histories. At the risk of creating a host of hospital bores McIndoe encouraged his patients to understand their operations. His patience in explaining each step proved good for morale as does good relations between enlightened management and the men and women on the factory floor. It also served practical purposes. Former Flight Lieutenant Laurence Chiswell wrote: "Although I am supposed to be finished, perhaps sometime you could drop my top lip on the left side which, as I pointed out at the last Guinea Pig Club weekend, has shrunk again somewhat since it was done three years ago."

During the war Richard Hillary employed the knowledge he had gained so painfully at the Sty to help

Britain at the highest diplomatic level in the United States. His problem was that after arriving there to lecture and broadcast during the summer of 1941, British Embassy officials complained that his appearance was too horrific. His plastic surgery was incomplete and the diplomatists took the view that Hillary could do more harm than good by appearing like that in an America which Winston Churchill was hoping to bring into the war.

Chagrined by this attitude, the young fighter pilot cabled McIndoe for permission to be operated upon by Dr Jerome Webster at the New York Medical Center. At the same time, at Hillary's request, Duff Cooper, Britain's Ambassador to Washington, cabled Sir Archibald Sinclair, the Liberal Air Minister in Churchill's wartime government, for his blessing on Hillary's activities.

Hillary was slabbed and afterwards he wrote to McIndoe:

> "I have to confess that I persuaded Webster considerably against his will to do a graft over the bridge of my nose between my eyes. I did this partly as a sop to official Washington which, as you may know, had been yammering for me to have my face done and partly because there has been some contraction of my left lower lid. My face is actually improved but as our officials here have such a bee in their bonnet about it, I doubt if they could ever be persuaded to notice the face unless I had some little job done."

Some guinea pigs visited the operating theatres more frequently as observers than as patients and improved the knowledge gained from discussion of their own operations by watching the plastic surgeons at work on their friends. It is, as any viewer of television hospital drama will appreciate, not the usual practice of hospitals to allow patients to wander in and out of the operating theatres in their dressing gowns. There was little that was usual about the Sty. Relatives, as with Jimmy Wright's father who watched surgery on his son from over McIndoe's shoulder, were welcome too.

McIndoe's readiness to encourage guinea pigs to observe operations was welcomed by Bill Simpson who was to write and philosophise about so much of what had happened to him. Bill stored clear images and memories of the daily drama of McIndoe's operating theatre; particularly the working rapport of Archie, his theatre sister Jill Mullins and John Hunter, his jovial anaesthetist – the magnificent trio who are remembered annually in the ritual reunion dinner toast "to Archie, John and Jill".

Bill noted at the time: "These three individuals are a perfect team and to watch them together in the theatre is to see a marvellous example of team work." He described Jill as dressed (as ever) in green, slender and with red-gold hair and extremely neat hands which were perfect for needlework on grafts and excised scars; and finishing off much of the surgeon's work. He depicted McIndoe in white shoes and light green cap and John Hunter at the patient's head and, in the words of the Guinea Pig anthem, 'running the gasworks'.

"Behind McIndoe's horn-rimmed spectacles there was a set look in his eyes. You could almost see him planning each successive move of the operation . . . the first incision was a masterly stroke quickly and firmly made with a scalpel. It left a pink line stretching from ear to ear around the patient's forehead. Soon the whole of the flesh and the skin of the forehead had been separated from the scalp and folded down, inside out, back over his eyes and nose. The hole in his skull was exposed."

Bill went on to describe the removal, using chisel and hammer, of a piece of bone from the patient's hip, its transfer to his forehead and the replacement of the flap of skin and flesh, neatly sewn with a long line of minute black stitches. He ended: "I left the theatre with a thrill of satisfaction running up and down my spine. I had seen the marvels of modern plastic surgery. I was encouraged beyond words by the realisation that the pair of firm, skilful hands which I had just seen operating would continue to operate on others and on me."

George Taylor, who went home to build a successful motor car agency in New South Wales, was one of the most badly injured among the boisterous fraternity of Australian pigs. He commented:

"Through watching many different types of plastic

surgery operations some of the pigs learned to be very selective when discussing with their surgeons the types of grafts they wanted. In the latter stages the boss used to allow me to write down the various jobs I wanted performed, so that we could talk over the list, discussing such things as whether I should have the Thiersch, Dermatome or Epidermoplasty between the fingers; or the pros and cons of Wolfe, Full Thickness, Partial Thickness, or Dermatome on the palms of the hands. Archie would sometimes indicate why a flap graft in a particular position would do the best job, but why another type as a compromise would be better because of the time factor.

"There was no such thing as him saying, 'Who's doing this job? You leave it to me.' On the contrary, he would treat those air force patients who chose to be interested as though they were a paying clientele with a competitive choice and seek their opinions as plainly as a shoe shop salesman."

After such consultations, George Taylor and his friends made out what they called their 'shopping list' and pinned it to the fronts of their operation smocks before being wheeled into the theatre. George's list always started by stating which hand he wished to be done. This was because he had had it agreed with the boss that once the hands were healed and beginning to be useful, it would be a calamity if, following an operation on both hands at once for the purpose of gaining extra movement, he contracted an infection in both hands simultaneously. Like men who have wobbled on the tightrope of financial disaster, the mutilated learn that it is wise to keep a reserve.

A guinea pig rediscovering the use of one hand after weeks of dependence, counted himself a veritable 'Lord of the Sty'. He needed a free hand, in any event, to grope for the shopping list upon surfacing from the anaesthetic. Each completed item would be neatly ticked and against the unfinished jobs, the surgeon had noted appropriate comments and explanations.

Familiarity invariably produced awkward situations. Such an intimate relationship between surgeons and patients proved a magnificent morale builder but it led to one especially delicate problem. Individual guinea pigs grew rather choosy about their surgeons. They recognised certain surgeons as being more skilled, say, at hands than noses, at eyelids than legs and they put themselves down for operations by specified surgeons, in accordance with a personal assessment of their abilities.

Much discussion of McIndoe's team and their individual talents took place in the wards and in the public houses of East Grinstead and generally the surgeons accepted this in good spirit and uncomplainingly. From time to time, however, visiting surgeons encountered an openly hostile distrust among their patients – and the perplexing phenomenon of a surgically astute pilot, navigator or air-gunner presenting his shopping list. Surgeons, however, reaped sufficient psychological and practical benefit from this unorthodox patient behaviour to neutralise the occasional awkward situation and overall the medical profession was to benefit from this unusual procedure.

A number of guinea pigs subsequently joined the profession. Tommy Brandon, who was an air-gunner when his Halifax crashed and exploded on landing, became the senior medical photographer at St Thomas' Hospital. Bertram Owen-Smith, helped by the club and the personal encouragement of Russell Davies and the boss, became a plastic surgeon. Additionally, medical knowledge born of the close relationship between guinea pigs and the Sty's medical staff, was to prove helpful in the pensions war. Appearing before a tribunal, John Taylor, suspecting that the club's case that his stomach ulcer was attributable to his RAF service was not going too well, paused to fumble in his pocket. With that touch of theatre, which is so much a feature of guinea piggery, he produced and explained the relevant and pickled portion of his inside.

CHAPTER FOUR

"As we worked a persistent question nagged at my mind: when their bodies are whole again can we also rebuild something of their lives?"

Bertram Owen-Smith left school at seventeen and a half and worked in an estate agent's office for six months until he was old enough to begin his training as a pilot. He did not possess the school certificate when the RAF accepted him, but he worked hard and was an operational pilot when the accident happened in which he lost a great deal of his face. His hands were burned too, but not beyond repair, and the surgical skills of McIndoe and his team enabled him to return to operational flying between surgical operations.

A number of guinea pigs indulged in this somewhat unusual form of occupational therapy and at stages in the war when operationally trained aircrew were at a premium the nation had cause to be grateful for the resumed services of a half-repaired guinea pig. Some, like Geoff Page and the Czech fighter pilot, Frankie Truhlar, returned to the Sty with new wounds.

Nevertheless, there were many long weeks when a pig had to lie in a ward and wait and it was during these weeks that Bertram Owen-Smith, the young estate agent's clerk from Swansea, nourished an ambition to become a plastic surgeon. He educated himself in bed and matriculated at the Sty. Nobody in the club thought he would ever qualify as a doctor and then as a surgeon. But the club stuck to its great principle that a member with an ambition should be given every opportunity to prove to himself that he could not achieve it. Financial help was provided. Owen-Smith became a doctor and a surgeon, worked under McIndoe at East Grinstead and eventually practised as a leading consultant in plastic surgery in southern Africa.

The early Maxillonians in Ward 3 would have raised an unbelieving roar had anybody suggested that the successors to their grogging club would some day manage to find the means to enable the training of a future plastic surgeon from among its members; that it would produce doctors, opticians, sanitary inspectors, accountants and trained men in many professions. Had there not been some difficulty in finding a pair of hands to uncork and pour the sherry on that sunny Sunday morning in 1941?

The roar of disbelief would have been heightened had anybody added forestry to the list of future guinea pig occupations. Nobody at the Queen Victoria Hospital really believed that Jock Duncan would one day stand before a tree with an axe in his hands. He had no fingers with which to grip the handle of an axe. If you clench your fists and look down at your knuckles, you will gain some understanding of what remained of Jock's hands. You may also agree with what even the maestro accepted at the time, that in applying to Jock the guiding principle of allowing a pig to discover for himself that he could not fulfil his ambition, the Guinea Pig Club would be encouraging the impossible.

From his bed, Jock told the surgeon: "I would like to become a forester." McIndoe replied: "I will do my best but it will necessitate additional operations on your hands and even then I cannot promise you that you will be able to hold an axe." The great principle was to be put to the test, irrespective of the cost in time and money. Nevertheless, if it comforted the young Scot, who had volunteered from his 15s. 0d. a week job as a village draper's assistant to fly with the air force, and faced a long series of surgical operations buoyed by a dream of great trees falling to his axe, then it was desirable that this flicker of hope be allowed him.

If you look at your fist again and feel down the top of your hands from the knuckle of each finger, you will discover something of which hitherto you may not have been particularly aware: your fingers begin near the wrist.

When McIndoe told Jock he would have to undergo additional operations, he had conceived the idea of contriving artificial clefts in the palms of the patient's hands. The operations took place. At intervals between them, McIndoe arranged for Jock to visit a forestry estate in Gloucestershire and to begin to get the feel of an axe, starting with a light five pounder.

The result was a successful and jubilant Jock Duncan. He married his nurse who was a South African girl and soon Russell Davies was writing to the burns committee of the RAF Benevolent Fund: "It was the opinion of everybody who met him that physically Jock Duncan would be unable to do manual labour in the open air by virtue of his extremely serious burns with residual of both face and hands. However, it was felt that he should be allowed to follow his inclination in order that he could prove to himself that he was unable to fulfil his wishes."

In 1950, Jock and his wife, assisted by the club, sailed for South Africa. The rest of their story is not so happy, partly because living in South Africa, Jock was beyond the reach of the regular assurance and encouragement of Blackie and Russell.

At first the couple seemed to be happy. Jock wrote: "I am very keen to settle here. The climate seems ideal for guinea pigs." But it did not take long for another aspect of South Africa to dispirit him. Wielding an axe was a black's job. Employers did not put it to Jock quite like that but whenever he applied for a manual job in forestry his "mitts", as he reported to the club, were viewed without sympathy and were possibly used as an excuse to prevent him working as a forester.

When, eventually, he found employment with a wool firm, it was not in the open air as he had hoped. He was, as a white had to be in the post-war Union of South Africa, an overseer of black labour. A wool slump put him out of work and the ensuing uncertainty which would have been distressing enough to an uninjured man disturbed Jock's mind. The Guinea Pig Club, observing with concern from a distance, was relieved when news arrived that he had found a new job in an oxygen plant. Unfortunately, he could not hold it down and when he left he deteriorated mentally.

Jock's parents made the long voyage from Scotland to the Cape to see their son and informed the club that in their opinion he would be restored to normal mental health if he returned home. Local medical opinion disagreed, assessing Jock as schizophrenic and dangerous.

This medical report confronted the club with a distressing dilemma. One of the last of McIndoe's actions on behalf of a guinea pig was to examine Jock's case with Russell Davies.

The facts were that if the club decided to find the money to bring him home – a costly measure because air travel and two male attendants were insisted upon by the South African authorities – then he would be separated from his wife and two children, perhaps forever.

His South African-born wife was willing to let her husband go if McIndoe considered a parting would be in his best interest, but she felt that she should stay in South Africa to bring up the children. Her family and roots were there. Jock Duncan never returned to Scotland. He was beyond decision on his own behalf and the club decided that he should be near his wife and family. He remained, withdrawn and solitary, in a South African mental hospital. Almost certainly the will of the young Scottish shop assistant who went to war and accepted additional operations to equip himself to earn a living as a forester, ran out when he was dismissed by the wool firm shortly before his fortieth birthday.

Possibly, there was, as Russell Davies believed, an underlying tendency towards schizophrenia. Whatever the reason for Jock's sad decline his experience underlined the wisdom of British-born guinea pigs who remained within reach of the club and its medical and welfare facilities. Not that his wife was neglected. The club kept in touch with her and helped to educate the children while she nursed in Pretoria.

* * *

Bill Foxley's body will never be whole again. He can see, but less than Nelson at Trafalgar. He wears one glinting, well-polished, meticulously matched glass eye in the right socket and sight only remains in one half of his left eye. He has a new, expressionless face, in which the most animate feature is the glass eye when the light catches it. His face is emotionless because fire destroyed skin, muscle, and everything facial up to the eyebrows with which Bill Foxley arrived in this world.

Surgeons can graft skin to cover the blackened, contracted mess of a man's face but they cannot always simulate a smile. They leave, as with some of the guinea pigs, a static clown-like grin. Bill Foxley's emotions, then, cannot be observed in the eyes or in the face. Nor can they be detected in the hands. Bill has no hands. But they are expressed, none the less, by the agitation of the scarred stumps which end where whole men's hands begin and by an increased rate of blink of his reconstructed eyelids.

When Bill Foxley dies he will not look his age. The youthful high spirits with which he sallied into aircrew have not left him and surgery has rendered him facially ageless. Only his hair betrays the advancing years. When one considers Bill's injuries, one immediately understands why even Blackie, the great optimist, feared that the club would have to face the prospect that Bill Foxley would be unemployable.

Yet, Bill Foxley became the house manager for a large Central Electricity Generating Board building. McIndoe was to say: "As we worked, a persistent question nagged at my mind: when their bodies are whole again can we also rebuild something of their shattered lives?" Given time much of Bill Foxley's shattered life was rebuilt – but only after years of personal endeavour and support from the Guinea Pig Club.

Reconstruction of his face nearing completion, Bill's high spirits persuaded him and those responsible for his welfare that, in common with many pigs, while he may have been maimed and disfigured, he remained a fit man.

Bill Foxley's body was as whole again as McIndoe and his surgeons could make it and he set out to show how fit a guinea pig could become. He went into athletic training, creating a fair reputation for himself as a runner before advancing years began to slow him down. He also married Cath, a very attractive East Grinstead girl who had worked in the hospital treasurer's office.

In passing, Bill was not alone among guinea pigs who

subsequently excelled in sport. The club's membership included former Flight Lieutenant Kim Hall, a golf professional and another Flight Lieutenant, Bob Graham, who having lost his eye and his right arm in a 1941 night flying accident, won the one armed golf championship ten years later. Bertram Owen-Smith played rugger for Westminster Hospital.

Athletic though he was, Bill Foxley's physical fitness was of little avail to him when he returned from the war to an ironmonger's shop. Fumbling for the nails and other sharp articles which are inevitable to that trade, the stumpy remains of his hands began to bleed.

Blackie was concerned and because sweets and tobacco are easier to handle than nails and nuts and bolts, Bill was helped to establish himself in Boutport Street, not many minutes from Blackie's home at Barnstaple. Bill and Cath worked hard at shopkeeping but even Bill will admit that he was not nature's best shopkeeper and in time the club decided to help him out of his shop and into a new occupation.

The final decision to rescue Bill recalls the great post-war debt owed by the Guinea Pig Club to Air Vice-Marshal Sir John Cordingley, the then Controller of the RAF Benevolent Fund, for his unflagging personal interest in its members' individual affairs. Sir John called on Bill's shop in Barnstaple and sensed that, with increased competition, all was not as well as it had been when government controls were still in force and Bill was receiving a fair share of supplies.

In the early days of peace one of the club's most useful services for its shopkeeping members was to help to alleviate the problems of scarcity. Thus, for instance, Blackie was to write to a toffee manufacturer on Bill's behalf: "I wonder if you can help this man by increasing his allocation of toffees. I can assure you that if you can manage this you will be assisting a most deserving man to take his place in the community again and in spite of his gross injuries to be an economic asset to the town in which he lives."

When finally Bill left the shop even Blackie worried privately that, with only half an eye, he might have to be accepted as unemployable, apart possibly from mouldering in one of the repetitive and unrewarding jobs customarily available to the disabled. Yet such is the spirit of guinea piggery, that for the rest of his working life former Warrant Officer Bill Foxley commuted daily between Crawley and London for his post with the Central Electricity Generating Board. In a nearby building a retired and whole air commodore held a similar position.

It was a fellow guinea pig, Sam Gallop, a sometime editor of the *Guinea Pig* magazine and Deputy Secretary of the Central Electricity Generating Board, who helped Bill into the career for which he proved himself as suited, if not more suited, than many whole men.

Sam first encountered Bill in 1943 when they occupied adjacent beds at East Grinstead. Bill was enveloped in white bandages. "The invisible man himself," Sam thought, "and then a voice emerged and revealed to me the important fact, 'you can get eggs here'."

While Sam Gallop was at the hospital he never saw Bill. Only the invisible man. In 1945 the pair were introduced at a party as strangers and it was then they discovered that they knew each other. Later Sam heard about Bill's difficulties and visited him in Barnstaple. Sam provided him with the opportunity of an interview. Bill went on, as Sam said,"to do a magnificent job and be promoted on merit." In the late 1960s he took a short break to make a fleeting appearance as a burned and disfigured pilot in the late 1960s feature film of the Battle of Britain.

Several guinea pigs became doctors, but there is only one doctor who became a guinea pig. While Owen-Smith's hands were repaired so that he could operate as a plastic surgeon when he had qualified, Noel Newman, already an RAF doctor, looked at his hands after the flames had roasted them in a desert air crash and knew that the fire had robbed him of all opportunity to become an orthopaedic surgeon as he had wished.

But being a doctor before he was burned did not spare 'Doc' Newman as he became known in the club from experiencing many of the same fears and misgivings of his fellow guinea pigs. Yet he was a guinea pig with a big difference in that his professional training led him to seek to investigate his reactions rather than to drown the horror in drink. He said:

"When you are first injured, and if in pain, you hope to
die. As soon as the drugs become effective or the pain
eases, you hope to live. The smallest things begin to
become something to live for. Even if it's only the Irish
stew for lunch. Then you begin to take the small things
for granted and the process continues."

At this point, Doc Newman discovered that many guinea
pigs – including himself – approached their greatest crisis:

"After weeks, perhaps months, of pampering
somebody says, 'Do it yourself.' The spoiling is over.
You are reckoned well enough to begin to do little
chores for yourself. And then you find you cannot do
them or they take patience and cause pain. Very
ordinary functions which men take for granted. Shoe
laces, fly buttons, tooth brushing. Even sipping a glass
of beer in bed. The distress at this point is savage, and
few are the guinea pigs whose pillows were not stained
by tears of bitterness."

Doc Newman believes that there were guinea pigs who
never overcame the crisis point and that they were to be
found among those who remained most in need of the club,
though some of them may not have remained closely in
touch with it.

* * *

Few members of the club rebuilt their lives in the air but
among them was Jackie Mann who became an airline
captain. On April 4, 1941, Jackie, a sergeant pilot who was
later commissioned, survived a crash landing in a blazing
No 91 Squadron Spitfire which was thought to have been
shot down by Major Adolf Galland, the German ace. It was
the sixth time he had been brought down, the five previous
occasions having occurred in 1940 during the Battle of
Britain.

On September 14, 1940, Jackie, flying with No 64
Squadron, gained his fourth life. His parents had been told
he had died from wounds in hospital after crash landing at
Hawkinge on the Kent coast, and turned up at the hospital
with a coffin to receive their son's remains. At the hospital
the mortuary keeper told Jackie's father: "We have several

pilots here and we don't know which of them is your son. Nobody would be able to tell. Frankly we don't mind which one you take." His father sought the police sergeant who had accompanied Jackie to the hospital and learned there had been a mistake. Jackie was alive and in a hospital bed.

Jackie was always thankful that in the course of spending his six lives he managed to crash land rather than bale out. It had been a salutary experience, he said, to circle protectively round a fellow fighter pilot who had baled out and whose body was on fire and at 1,000 feet suddenly dropped clear of his parachute harness. He said: "Whether he released himself or whether the fire had burned him out of the harness I never discovered. But at the moment his body fell away to the ground black smoke was curling up from his seat, up his back and round his neck. One of many airmen who did not live to become a guinea pig."

Twenty-one years afterwards, Jack Mann who had become a Comet Captain with Middle East Airlines wrote to Tom Gleave:

> "That I have reason to be grateful, oh inadequate word, to Archie McIndoe, is readily evident from the following quotation from *Tally Ho (Yankee in a Spitfire)* by Arthur Gerald Donahue.
>
> 'Two of the boys had been badly wounded and at least one of them, Sergeant Mann, is not expected to fly again. He was awarded the Distinguished Flying Medal while in the hospital. This boy had been shot down for the sixth time. His machine was badly shot up and his engine wrecked over the Channel but he managed to glide back over land. Then, when he was only two hundred feet up, too low to bale out, his machine caught fire and he had to force land it in a farmer's field.
>
> 'He crawled out of the cockpit then and in spite of the fact that he was terribly burned, he took his camera out of his pocket, carefully adjusted it for light and distance and snapped the pictures of the blazing wreck, after which he staggered across two fields to the farm house.'"

Donahue, one of the American volunteers who flew in the Battle of Britain, failed to survive much longer. After destroying a Ju 88 bomber he ditched in the Channel. Rescue launches searched in vain.

Captain Jack Mann continued his letter to Tom, the chief guinea pig: "Art Donahue, unfortunately, did not live to see the day the boss would prove the pundits wrong; at the time of writing, some fifteen thousand flying hours wrong." Balancing Donahue's account he wrote:

"On April 4th, 1941, I began the day as a sergeant pilot of 91 Squadron, operating from Hawkinge and ended it by being reborn a guinea pig in a field at Paddlesworth, Kent, within sight of Hawkinge.

"After some time – days being sightless and timeless – in the Royal Victoria Hospital, Folkestone (I have an idea it was ten to fourteen), I was told I was being removed to East Grinstead. In my abysmal ignorance I rebelled at being moved so abruptly from the vicinity of my birthplace but I went – and arrived and into a saline bath. And more saline baths until such time as, fragment by fragment, the suppurating leather skin formed by copious applications of tannic acid, could be cut by scalpel from my legs. And until such time as the scar tissue around my eyes had reached a stage where the maestro could say: 'You are for the slab this morning Jackie.' Then my protest: 'But my people are coming to see me this morning' and his inimitable response: 'Oh, we'll have you back by then' and his instructions to John Hunter, his highly regarded aide and anaesthetist: 'Just keep him under, he has visitors coming.'"

Following the war guinea pigs were generally reticent about recounting their experiences to one another let alone outsiders and Jackie Mann's letter to Tom Gleave had been unusually, if not fully communicative. The passage of time was to weaken this once strong inhibition which derived partly from not wishing to appear to be 'shooting a line'.

Jackie was to expand his tale of how he became a guinea pig. He said he had been ordered up from Hawkinge with Sergeant A.W.P. Spears, a nephew of McCudden the First

World War RFC fighter ace, to intercept two enemy aircraft approaching the Kent harbour of Ramsgate. After a while the pair were told the enemy had gone home and so they relaxed. It was then that the enemy, still very much around, shot down Spears and hit his aircraft with some fifteen cannon shells. Jackie had selected a field for a forced landing when he noticed there was a great deal of petrol in the cockpit but at less than 400 feet it was too late to bale out.

Jackie remembered: "All I could do was close my eyes and hold the plane as it was going." The cockpit caught fire and he landed with his eyes shut. The starboard wing which had been hit by cannon fire fell off on impact and killed two sheep. Dazed, Jackie decided that he had come down in France and was consumed by a fear that had haunted him since listening as a child to an uncle's memories of being a prisoner of war in Germany. At all costs he must evade capture.

Attempting to beat out his burning clothes he returned to the cockpit to retrieve his parachute and hurled it into a ditch, aiming to hide it and make the enemy think he had baled out miles away. Crossing two fields Jackie came to a cottage where instead of the French farm wife he had expected to answer his knock, he encountered an elderly English lady. Seeking to comfort him she said: "I am so sorry you have experienced such a horrid motor-cycle accident", went for her bicycle, and pedalled away to fetch a doctor.

After a year Jackie resumed flying. When in 1943 he received a posting to a ground job in India his recently married wife contacted McIndoe urgently: "Take him off flying", she urged, "and he will blow up." The posting was cancelled and Jackie completed his war as a transport pilot.

This was the very same Jack Mann who eventually retired from airline captaincy to settle in Beirut and manage the Duke of Wellington bar in the Marble Towers Hotel, and later the Pickwick Bar before on May 12, 1989, he was kidnapped and held hostage. News of his release on September 24, 1991, reached Tom Gleave three days before the club's fiftieth anniversary lost weekend during which Tom called Jackie at RAF Lyneham where he was being debriefed and recuperating. Their conversation was relayed to the assembled guinea pigs. Afterwards the Manns made a new home in Cyprus where Jackie learned that he had been appointed CBE.

Another guinea pig whose story took a long time to surface was John 'Paddy' Gingles who flew with No 617, the celebrated Dambusters Squadron *after* surgery at the Queen Victoria Hospital and enrolment as a member of the club. Paddy, who was from Larne in Northern Ireland, was seventeen and under age when he enlisted. In the autumn of 1941 and making his fifth trip of an eventual total of 71 bomber operational sorties Sergeant Pilot Gingles, flying a No 9 Squadron Wellington in a raid on Emden, had almost reached home when the bomber crashed and, thrown forty yards from the wreckage, he was the sole survivor of its six-man crew.

Following plastic surgery Paddy resumed operations with another Wellington squadron, until April 1944, when he was posted as a flying officer to No 617. Temporarily based some twenty miles from the Arctic port of Archangel he turned out for a somewhat scratch RAF football eleven against a Russian side at Yagodnik, 617's airfield on the Dvina river. Soon after a well-trained Soviet Naval Air Force team, aided it was thought by a future Moscow Dynamo goalkeeper, scored a seven nil victory, 617's Lancasters made an abortive attack on the battleship *Tirpitz* lying in Norway's Alten fjord. *Tirpitz* moved to a shallow anchorage at Tromso where on November 13, 1944, the Dambusters squadron, operating this time from Lossiemouth in Scotland, made a further attack and one of Paddy's bombs – he reported "we think we obtained a direct hit"- was reckoned to have helped to capsize the battleship. Paddy completed his war as a flight lieutenant with a DFC and an earlier DFM and served into the early 1950s when he began a long career as a captain with Dan Air, flying finally with Pakistan International.

There were, of course, exceptions to the general post-war reticence of the majority of guinea pigs to tell their stories among themselves. Richard Hillary, Bill Simpson, Richard Pape and Geoffrey Page were among those who wrote books; and Paul Hart, whose Lincolnshire bulb-growing business was boosted by Wilfred Pickles on BBC radio's *Have A Go* programme. Collie Knox, the *Daily Mail* columnist followed up: "Good luck to the bulb grower. I hope he makes a million for Sir Stafford Cripps [Chancellor in the post-war Labour government] to take away from him."

But, save such examples, the majority of guinea pigs knew little of each other's exploits excepting such Sty hilarities as the attempted ducking of Ward 3's popular and legendary Sister Meally or the wheelchair chariot races down the steep hill which leads from East Grinstead towards the hospital.

Thus, asked to send the chief guinea pig details of his experiences in and out of hospital former Flight Lieutenant Brian Birks, DFC – he was station aircraft safety officer when he walked into a turning propeller – wrote: "Most memorable experience: Admission to Ward 3 to the accompaniment of female shrieks and the sight of a battered pyjama-clad patient carrying the immaculately uniformed ward sister towards a bath of cold water."

Or Jack Toper's matter of fact response:

> "29th August, 1943. Crash landed Clacton-on-Sea (bombs gone of course). D Day, 1944, saw yours truly sharing a room at Marchwood Park with twenty other types. This was the beginning of doodlebugs. One of the room mates was more than concerned with his second degree burns on his mitts. Came the night. Doodles falling around. Bedroom door closed. A handle to turn. We were watching the fireworks. Suddenly a doodlebug cut out above us. There was a mad rush to the door to belt down to the basement. We found (at least two of us did) the door was too difficult to open. We had vision of unpleasant happenings. Lo and behold, the chap with the poor mitts opened the door and we all made our escape. Thereafter, he didn't have a leg to stand on."

The last sentence was underlined by Jack who continued:

> "Following a visit to the slab in conjunction with my rhino pedicle (for the ignoramus, a new nose) was residing in the Canadian wing. The day after I was jissing around the ward with a charming French

Canadian sister, feeling pleased with life at the prospect of a new trunk. That night it was action stations. I had a haemorrhage. The Guinea Pig dinner (1944) was two days away. Yes, I missed it. Blackie commiserated and supplied me with a whole chicken as compensation. When the chicken arrived, to my astonishment, I was the most popular man in the wing. That's right. The types helped me to eat it. They left me the parson's nose."

Some years afterwards when he had become a Marks and Spencer branch manager and editor of *Guinea Pig*, the club's magazine, Jack Toper asked fellow guinea pigs to contribute to a 'How I became a guinea pig' series. Reluctant to include himself he persuaded Pat Knight, skipper of the No 166 Squadron Wellington bomber in which he was burned, to tell his story. Pat wrote:

"I can't remember whether he selected me as his skipper or I chose him for his keenness and undoubted skill as a wireless operator . . . After a few ops we were detailed to deliver a load of incendiaries to Munchen Gladbach and this turned out to be our last flight together.

"We had climbed to about 16,000 feet when suddenly, without any warning the starboard engine blew up with the hell of a bang and within a split second we were hurtling earthwards in a spin which took a few minutes and several thousand feet to recover from. Having regained full control, we resumed normal flying and set a course for England.

"During the homeward flight we were attacked by a fighter and lost a few more thousand feet in a series of improvised evasive tactics and as the enemy coast was crossed we had a ding-dong battle with coastal defences. There was no alternative other than to dive to sea level. On one engine and lots of hope we resumed our course of 270 degrees. During the North Sea crossing I instructed Jack and other members of the crew to jettison every item, including parachutes, in order to assist the now labouring engine as every pound was vital.

"After a lifetime the UK coastline became visible and never was there a louder cheer. As we had not much idea of our position we planned to carry out a series of eliptical orbits of the coastline till dawn and then find a nice friendly drome. One of our crew suggested ditching just off the coast but as I had read just two days before of a Lanc crew who had ditched off the east coast quite safely, climbed into their dinghy then had the terrible misfortune to collide with one of our anti-invasion devices – with no survivors – this did not appeal.

"At this point we had inched our way up to 300 feet but as the engine was labouring in a most protesting manner we ignited a wing tip flare and just as we saw with horror that a town was below the engine burst into flames, leaving a space of about three seconds for the crew to take up crash stations."

The Wellington struck a tree and burst into flames. All the crew were injured, pilot and wireless operator seriously. They were pulled out of the wreckage by nearby anti-aircraft gunners. Jack's burns were worse than they might have been. One of the crew had failed to jettison his parachute and the crash impact had opened it blocking his escape. Jack's eventual exit was described as "like a living candle emerging from the plane with flames six foot high from his face."

Some time afterwards when his skipper offered him and his wife, Sybil, a lift to a squadron reunion Jack smiled: "No thanks old chap. Look what happened to me last time you gave me a lift." In a footnote to his skipper's account Jack noted: "Flying home on that fateful night Pat received shrapnel wounds to his leg and although he was in great pain and at one stage I had to hold his leg to the rudder, he insisted on flying our mortally wounded aircraft himself. When we crashed he was flung out of the cockpit, broke a leg and punctured his lung. So fellow guinea pigs I have not broken ranks by printing my own story. It appears as a tribute not only to a superb pilot but also to an exceptional man."

When Tom Gleave asked Francis 'Dixie' Dean for his best rehabilitation story Dixie wrote:

"There were so many. One I recall was while I was at Marchwood Park. A crowd of us were invited to the local ATS (Auxiliary Territorial Service) mess for a do. Lashings of grog and girls. However towards the end, namely midnight, Dixie was missing. The guards were called out to search all the girls' billets and beds – they knew where to look as they thought. Alas, they could not find me. They did in the end in an ATS sergeant's bed *alone* with a black eye and to this day I do not know how I got it except I've got a photo of an ATS sergeant and written on the back is the following.

'Here's to the aircrew boy with the auburn hair,
Who got a black eye,
Through taking a dare!'"

CHAPTER FIVE

"Social disability is by far the greatest handicap."

The Guinea Pig Club is registered as an official war charity for tax purposes. Here, however, in the non-biblical sense of a misused word ends any connection between the club and charity. McIndoe detested the word charity and all the anachronistic nineteenth century attitudes associated with it; attitudes embodied in the belief that the British Empire would flourish so long as there were flag days, garden parties, fetes, jumble sales and an annual ex-servicemen's 'Not Forgotten Association' tea at Buckingham Palace.

Charitable organisation in name, then, because fifty to sixty years ago an establishment awaiting its routine honours would not have understood an avant garde charity which disowned the concept of charity. The Guinea Pig Club neither canvassed charitable support nor administered charitable funds in the accepted sense of the word and this was a process it disdained.

Having, at the Queen Victoria Hospital, as he wrote in the postgraduate Medical Journal in 1943, "removed the institutional atmosphere which is the curse of much hospital life", McIndoe named charity his second enemy and worked to protect his guinea pigs from it.

Persistently he sought to divert guinea pigs from institutions or from the generally menial and poorly paid jobs allocated to disabled service people and to launch them into competitive life knowing that often the physical effort might prove too arduous. Always he insisted "Exhaust *all* sources before dealing with the matter as a charity." Frequently he preached "a guinea pig should be a useful member of the community and not playing a cornet in Piccadilly."

Welcome and well-meaning though McIndoe's mantra was, his stance against alms compelled some of the former airmen into competitive occupations in which the stress told sooner or later. But McIndoe argued it was better to risk a need to resort to charity later in life than condemn a guinea pig to unvarying years of enforced helplessness, knitting and rug-making an institutionalised life away; disciplined as if mental because the burns of war had made him different from those who would hide him away.

McIndoe's creed endowed the club with a future responsibility which was to test it demandingly in the future as guinea pigs aged and their disabilities increased the usual problems of growing older. In fact, acceptance of this likelihood was of course potentially less onerous in the light of the club's close association with the RAF Benevolent Fund which Sir Winston Churchill called: "part of the conscience of the British nation". Indeed, Sir Winston had alluded, albeit unintentionally, to the future significance of the fund's accord with the Guinea Pig Club when shortly after the war he broadcast: "It is our duty now to make sure that the Fund will be able to go on helping, and not fail as the survivors of the war grow old and feeble."

Growing old and feeble as a guinea pig meant failing sight when you have only half an eye, or if you are more fortunate one eye; rheumatic fingers – if you had any – on stumpy hands. Executively, such problems were and continue to be met by the decisions of the Burns Committee which connects the 'Ben Fund' and the club and for the introduction of which the club will ever remain especially indebted to Air Vice-Marshal Sir John Cordingley, Controller of the RAF Benevolent Fund in the post-war period.

There was never, it should perhaps be explained, any contradiction between acceptance of assistance for individual members from the Benevolent Fund and the Guinea Pig Club's abhorrence of charity. The issue remains that there is no connection between the club and charity as the flag-buying public conceives it. The RAF Benevolent Fund is, as Sir Winston said, "part of the conscience of the British nation". Whether disbursed by loan or by grant, Fund assistance is the delayed acknowledgement of former service and sacrifice.

A guinea pig fighter pilot, 'fried' in a Spitfire during the Battle of Britain, endorsed this reasoning when he made an at the time anonymous broadcast appeal on behalf of the RAF Benevolent Fund. He said: "The Battle of Britain meant my facing the fact that I should never use my hands again and that I was burned and scarred for life. For a time I didn't even want to live. That is what despair does. The RAF Benevolent Fund convinced me that I could start again in a life of my own choosing – and assisted me with means to do it."

This guinea pig who didn't want to live became headmaster of his own private and flourishing preparatory school in Surrey. He was Peter Weeks, the Maxillonian, who had been elected secretary of the Ward 3 grogging club because, in that moment of hospital hilarity, it seemed appropriate to appoint a secretary who could not write and might never write again.

* * *

There was a distinction between the long-term help the RAF Benevolent Fund could provide from its deep purse and the generally shorter term loans and gifts within the limited resources of the Guinea Pig Club. Apart from some larger loans made shortly after the war to assist some members to begin commercial or professional lives the club, leaning on the Benevolent Fund for substantial sums, concentrated upon the provision of first-aid to defeat the depressions of social disability. Here, also, there can be found no definable charitable process through which the Guinea Pig Club held out and continues to proffer a helping hand. Its actions, between the annual lost weekend pep mixture of boisterous goodwill, physical, mental and welfare stocktaking and alcoholic bonhomie, have always been prompted not by any written constitution but by McIndoe's uncompromising dictum: "Social disability is the greatest handicap." In the years following the first meeting of the Maxillonians in Ward 3 the club's modest resources were devoted mainly to reducing that handicap. Since then welfare expenditure has sometimes been sufficiently exotic to ensure that the spirit of 1940 and 1941 has not been forgotten and that the club continues to

supply a unique service which, with the best will in the
world, no rule-ridden and stereoptyped 'charitable'
organisation could achieve. For instance, which normal
charity would accept that a "course of a week's
night-clubbing with plenty of money in his pocket", as
granted to a guinea pig, was considered the only treatment
likely to return a certain socially disabled guinea pig to
circulation.

Shocking use of a registered charity's funds? It worked,
and while there can be no proof, it is probable that this
enlightened hand-out at the critical moment saved its
recipient from many years in an institution at the expense
of the taxpayers for whom he had fought. Naturally, this
type of humanitarian therapy remained reasonably
confidential in the club's early years. The last thing Blackie
needed was a barrage of reversed charge calls pleading
with the headmaster of Barnstaple Secondary Modern for a
therapeutic night on the town – though he was always
available.

In the past sixty years the occasional inspired handout
generally originated from the sixth sense which long
experience of guinea piggery had developed in the brains
of the boss, Russell, Blackie and their successors. A fiver
here, a case of whisky there. A tenner. A coat for the winter,
a night out . . .

Blackie to Archie July 25th, 1951: "You remember the
suggestion with regard to X? I am sending form made out
£10 which I should like you to send him with your good
wishes to enable him to enjoy a good holiday. I have reason
to believe that he would enjoy this more than a case of
whisky as I first suggested. Will you write a note that
Harvey [treasurer] can send with the cheque?" X later
prospered as an executive in an oil company.

Blackie to Archie November 27, 1952: "I have had a long
letter from Y explaining the position with regard to his
child who, you may know, was born a mongol. At the
present time he is paying £3.17.6. a week for the child to be
boarded out. This is well beyond his income capacity and I
think the club will be doing a good job if I send him a
cheque for £50."

Although such thoughtful acts may seem trivial
alongside the club's pension battles, or say, the long-term

project to process a poorly educated air-gunner into a school teacher, they renewed confidence when it had reached its lowest mark and kept guinea pigs in the competitive world who otherwise might have deteriorated into even more problematical people.

There are, however, more ways of pulling a man up than reassuring him with kind words and cash handouts and the Guinea Pig Club never hesitated at dropping the fairy godmother's wand and wielding a broad cudgel when theatrical ferocity was considered necessary. But after the cudgel the hand holding was ever ready to follow a guinea pig's recovery of sense with kindness and where appropriate, cash.

To a guinea pig thrice jailed the boss would write harshly. To a solicitor about the same member: "I have borne with this young man's troubles for twenty-two years and I do not suppose that we shall ever come to an end of them." Blackie blasting another guinea pig:

> "We have spent an enormous amount of time and trouble over your re-settlement and it's most depressing to receive an unsatisfactory report of your work with. . . . The impression I gathered was that you are just not putting your back into your work but I am told further that you are hoping to get a grant from the RAF Benevolent Fund to start yourself in a grocery business. Let me say at once that, so bad has been our experience with you in relation to a business of any kind run by yourself, that under no circumstances would I support this application."

After reminding this guinea pig of his "easier opportunity to attain that position of respect in the community which most men who have been through what you have been through do easily command", Blackie wrote a kind letter to his employers, hoping that they would bear with him and give him another chance. He told a legless guinea pig: "Pull your socks up, even if they are on tin legs."

* * *

It was remarkable, considering the competitive push and shove and selfish personal endeavour of the post-war years, that such effort on behalf of individual guinea pigs should have continued. It would almost certainly not have done so had not the boss, Russell and Blackie remained intimately involved long, long after they could have honourably released themselves from almost daily attention to matters arising from their wartime duties. Far from making the excuse of new personal and professional responsibilities which would have been understood, the trio deepened the well of their involvement, providing guinea pigs in need a close and personal continuity of assurance and encouragement which was exceptionally fatiguing in conjunction with their own busy professional lives.

Bill Foxley's installation as a shopkeeper on Blackie's doorstep was an example of the extent of this commitment. McIndoe was even prepared, without notice, to take a guinea pig into his home. He knew that proximity to the source of confidence could mean the difference between hope and despair to a man not long deprived of the shelter of the Sty and the self-explanation of an air force uniform. He recognised that some guinea pigs required periodic shots of confidence.

Among McIndoe's closest relationships with a former patient was his care of Johnny Hills who remained for many months at his home and was employed to drive his Rolls-Royce car, enabling him to spend much time with the surgeon as he drove him to appointments and social engagements. Possibly, McIndoe was familiar with Rudyard Kipling's story, 'The Tender Achilles'. And perhaps the story had inspired Johnny's recruitment. Kipling wrote of two surgeons who were exchanging anecdotes. One surgeon, recalling a wartime operation upon a soldier, tells another that when the soldier was convalescent he was approached by him with an offer to become his chauffeur. But only he, the surgeon, knew that he had removed one-third of the man's brain!

Corporal Hills – who had not undergone brain surgery – had been working in a hangar when a bomb hit it and petrol tanks exploded. His broken and burned body was recovered from the wreckage. As a member of groundcrew, he was ordinarily ineligible for membership of the club, but no true guinea pig could contemplate Johnny without the utmost compassion and he was accepted without demur.

Beyond his injuries, and few guinea pigs know this, there was an even more compelling reason why Johnny needed the club. Lying for weeks in his hospital bed he had had the time to wonder where he could find the answers to two questions which, in his physical distress, were large and frightening.

Who was he? Where was he born? Johnny Hills had never known. Turning detective, Russell Davies brought peace to Johnny's mind. His mother had died during his father's war with the Germans, and his father had not come home. But, as Russell discovered, Johnny had a twin sister and Corporal Hills was thus enabled to look forward to a civilian future with an equanimity that might have eluded him for ever.

Johnny Hills had been in private service before the war. When his strength had returned, he began to consider the prospect of a new life abroad. His mother was dead, his father had disappeared, but having established his antecedents, he sought the club's assistance in satisfying this wish. As a patient at the Sty he had met Geoff Page's father-in-law, Nigel Bruce, who had appeared as the actor Basil Rathbone's fruity Dr Watson in Hollywood's pre-war Sherlock Holmes films.

Nigel Bruce had been admitted by McIndoe for an operation on an old wound of the First World War and now McIndoe, with Bruce's support, wrote to the British Consul-General in Los Angeles recommending Johnny as a butler, preferably within the Hollywood community. Alternatively Johnny inquired on his own account about emigration to Australia. He took that option and sailed down under with the club's assistance and blessing, built up a window-cleaning and lawn-mowing round at Adelaide in South Australia and earned a reasonable living.

Sometime afterwards Blackie and Russell were discussing guinea pig business at Blackie's home when their conversation was interrupted by the arrival of a postman with a letter from Johnny Hills containing news of his children. David, two, Ann, four, Peter, six, were doing well. But the big news was that he had just adopted a thirteen-year-old boy *to save him from having to grow up in an institution*, a decision arising directly from the Guinea Pig Club's founding raison d'etre.

Johnny wrote also of Jack Wishart, a fellow guinea pig who lived locally. – "Jack has been worried and it crossed my mind that, maybe, the club can help him." Johnny explained that Jack now had three children and that, his old leg wound having broken down, his wife was working in a store. Jack, he said, would never dream of asking but could not his forty per cent disability pension be reviewed in these circumstances?

Blackie handed the letter to Russell. "Yours", he said. "Can do?" "Sure." Johnny's letter from Australia and Blackie and Russell's brief exchange represented a practical expression of everything the Guinea Pig Club stood for and a guarantee for its future function as the union McIndoe intended it to be.

* * *

Although the boss, Blackie and Russell were in their lifetimes the most leaned upon stanchions of the club, this statement would be off balance without tribute to other guinea pig supporters who, while not in such close and regular touch with such a broad swathe of the membership, carried their wartime connection forward and remained supportive for the rest of their lives. They had been close enough to individual guinea pigs as they endured various stages of surgery, convalescence and resettlement in civilian life to understand and help combat the menace of social disability, making guinea pigs welcome in their homes and restoring self confidence.

Some guinea pigs gravitated to surgeons Jerry Moore and Percy Jayes, to McIndoe's wife, Connie, and to Elaine Blond, who, with her husband Neville, later paid substantially to establish the McIndoe Memorial Research Unit at the Sty and to Elise and Douglas Stern whose hospitality was prodigious, to name but some of the East Grinstead and Felbridge residents who rallied round during the war and remained friends of the Guinea Pig Club for ever and a day.

Had it not been for the war and the chance which brought McIndoe's Army to East Grinstead, such comfortably off people would not have known and had the opportunity to develop great affection for some guinea pigs who had entered life with few advantages, fought for their country and suffered horrendous consequences.

In pre and early post-war Britain, apart from the lady bountifuls and charity supporters, people of means were unlikely to mix with those who could count themselves lucky if they received a weekly wage packet; in no part of the home counties were the taboos and distinctions so prevalent as in the homes and gardens which the wealthy had built among the salubrious pinewoods along the Surrey and Sussex borders. Servants from the industrial north still staffed a household for a few shillings a week and their keep.

Like Johnny Hills, the one guinea pig the Sterns took in was another airman who could not offer the charisma of a Richard Hillary. He was not aircrew, a square little fellow from Manchester, indistinguishable from thousands of other square little north countrymen who helped England and were demobilised without very much to thank her for. Indistinguishable that was, until the RAF gave 'Little' George Hindley a balloon to care for, presenting a scene with all the pathos of a Stanley Holloway monologue.

They were winding in the balloon and George was guiding the great heavy cable which swung earthwards like a giant lead from a rogue elephant when it was carried into a high tension cable. Blackie remembered that when they brought Little George to East Grinstead Archie took one look at him and said "he ought to be dead". He was terribly burned and across the top of his head there ran a cleft, deep like a Pennine railway cutting and burned to more than the thickness of the cable. When George Hindley began to attend the annual lost weekends he was no longer indistinguishable from thousands of other north countrymen. Annually, he attended the lost weekend at East Grinstead where he joined Group Captain Tom Gleave, the chief guinea pig, as an honoured and fellow guest at the Stern's house party.

At the 1955 dinner, Archie McIndoe congratulated his Army: "The impressive line of expensive cars parked outside indicates that the club has a number of prosperous members. The number of chaps who roll up in Jaguars at guinea pig dinners is encouraging." Although it was not a Jaguar, Little George also had a car. The Guinea Pig Club had helped him to buy it so that he could continue to reach his work as a watchman until ill-health enforced his retirement.

* * *

The Guinea Pig Club's debt to Archie's, Russell's and Blackie's consistent caring involvement will now be clear, but they would wish it explained that the benefits were not one-sided. McIndoe's fashionable cosmetic practice thrived after the war in the sun of the unique personal publicity which notwithstanding medical ethics the nature of the Guinea Pig Club made permissible.

If Russell Davies, with his selfless approach to medicine, deliberately and correctly avoided plentiful opportunities for financial gain and fought shy of personal publicity, he was rewarded by ever increasing professional esteem at home and abroad. Of the trio, however, Blackie's war years at the Queen Victoria Hospital produced the least expected results. East Grinstead friendships and McIndoe's introductions led the Barnstaple schoolmaster into the higher reaches of entertainment, education, re-settlement and rehabilitation where his creative ideas and forceful character were in much demand.

Macmillan, the publishing house, appointed him consultant on educational books and he advised the English Stage Company at London's Sloane Square theatre on its selection of plays. While privately he advised Marks and Spencer, whose founding families were so closely involved with the Guinea Pig Club, he refused an offer of the post of Personnel Director, insisting on keeping his feet on the ground at Barnstaple Secondary Modern, remaining true to his vocation and building a happy family life with his beloved wife Joan and their children.

Archie, Russell and Blackie . . . it is tempting to quote a comment from Bill Bourn, a guinea pig writing from Ndola on the border of the former Northern Rhodesia – now Zambia: "Frankly, I formed the opinion that the patients were rehabilitating the staff."

* * *

All the fingers of Alan Morgan, who will be remembered from Chapter Three, were black and leathery. Horrible. When Ella, the Manchester girl Alan married and gave two sons to, visited the Sty, Alan's black fingers were ugly and frightening as they protruded from the contrastingly white bandages on his hands. "Like dried bananas", Ella said. Alan was a skilled man whose skill depended on the mobility of his hands.

He need not have worn uniform because, as a jig-borer and a young man who had served an apprenticeship, he was in a reserved occupation. He discovered just how much of a key man his country considered him to be when he volunteered for the Royal Navy and was told that his presence on the shop floor was too valuable for him to go to sea.

Disappointed, Alan waited until ever increasing bomber losses and the pressing need for crews to sustain 'Bomber' Harris's offensive against Germany eased the rules and he was permitted to volunteer to train for aircrew. The RAF converted him into a flight engineer and he was posted to a Lancaster squadron. On his thirteenth trip, and on the eve of his twenty-first birthday, Alan earned his guinea pig badge and tie through frost rather than fire.

At twenty-one, and contemplating a lifetime as a civilian, the sight of his useless fingers created deep fears in Alan's mind. His skill and the living he could earn through it, depended on his hands and, as he or anybody else would have supposed, it would not be possible for him to return to industry. It worried Ella too though she gave no hint of this to Alan whose natural anxiety increased when he learned that, despite all the efforts of McIndoe and his team at the Queen Victoria Hospital, his fingers would have to come off.

There had always been a glimmer of hope while they were still there, but the day came when the maestro had to tell him that they were for 'the chop'; a decision rendered all the more distressing because in the maestro's opinion Alan's fingers could have been saved had they received the correct treatment for frostbite at the hospital which had received him after the Lancaster's emergency landing.

Ella visited Alan frequently, making many journeys from Manchester to East Grinstead, and on one trip she brought her fourteen-year-old sister. "Whatever you do", she told her, "don't stare at any of the guinea pigs. Don't make them think you see anything peculiar about them." At the same time, Ella repeatedly reminded Alan how fortunate he was compared with most of his friends in the ward, some of whom had lost much of their faces and all or part of their eyesight.

Talking with other guinea pigs Ella discerned that Alan possessed another advantage. Whereas their all too brief operational careers had deprived them of opportunities to develop firm and stable relationships, Ella and Alan's romance had produced the expectancy of early marriage. Ella knew instinctively that as Alan's wife she could accelerate his rehabilitation putting him far ahead of some of the wild, unattached men who formed the hard core of the club's boozing fraternity. Yet what she could not know all those years ago was that however tenderly and lovingly she could help Alan to return to civilian life, his war-inflicted trauma and disability would in some circumstances stress him intolerably.

Alan's crisis moment came when the industrial company to which he had returned after the RAF had released him was taken over and he became unemployed. It had meant everything to Alan to be as good as the next man on the shop floor in paying his way as a fully-functioning member of society. Alan had worked with his hands, however grotesque the manipulation of his stumps might appear as they darted and prodded and pushed, and had achieved astonishing dexterity.

He had convinced his employer that not only could he function fully as a jig-borer but also as a very good jig-borer. For months after his surgical operations he had practised and practised using what remained of one thumb on one hand and half a thumb on the other. He had started by wearing out pencil after pencil to write his name over and over again until he was sick of the sight of it and would have gladly changed it. Apart from his thumb-and-a-half, the only help he had were the shallow clefts Archie McIndoe and his team had contrived for him as they had also done to help Jock Duncan realise his hospital ambition of seeing great trees fall to his axe.

Afterwards, Alan had trained himself to use what

remained of his hands with such determination that he believed that given a chance to persuade a medical board he could return to aircrew service for long enough to gain his promotion from sergeant to flight sergeant before demobilisation.

Alan told the maestro: "I'd like another bash in the air before it's too late." McIndoe said: "OK, providing you can sell your hands to the Air Ministry." Alan passed the board and was airborne again, flying between Britain and Gibraltar as a flight engineer. Back in civilian life, Alan's pre-war firm took a similar view as the RAF, welcomed him back and appreciated the importance he placed on achieving the highest of standards. He settled contentedly into a peacetime routine of factory work.

For her part, Ella had established a general store and even in the post-war years of continued rationing, managed to keep it well stocked thanks to helpful letters sent by the Guinea Pig Club to her suppliers. In time, Alan became so convincingly re-settled at work that Ella felt able to sell the shop and devote herself to her children, her home, and her husband.

And then the blow fell. Ella's sense of all being well was shattered when Alan's company was taken over in a City coup which in the nature of such acts took no account of the heartbreak it might produce in the Morgan home. Redundancy cash paid with a final week's wages was no compensation for the years of effort Alan Morgan had expended to negate the damage he had received while fighting to save his country and for that matter his employer's business.

Alan Morgan received fair notice of his dismissal, but the shock resulted in a serious nervous breakdown when he discovered that prospective new employers were cordial at interviews – until they saw his hands. They could not believe that his skill was not only unimpaired, but enhanced by his determination to show himself more proficient than his fellows. Nor would they trouble to put his protestations to the test. Worse, his former firm denied him a reference. Had Archie McIndoe been alive and had he heard how Alan had been treated a river of managerial blood would have flown through Manchester.

As it was Alan bottled up his distress. In his confusion he

had no idea how much the club could have helped him, or of the pressure it was prepared to exert to obtain justice in such cases. He went downhill and by the time the club discovered something was amiss he was too ill to explain his problems.

Alan Morgan's experience illuminates the one inevitable and major disadvantage of the Guinea Pig Club's loose-knit network which depended upon the as-and-when, and often intuitive attention of leaders, who were busily leading the new lives they had made since their wartime and wholetime association with the guinea pigs.

Neither Alan nor Ella understood how forcefully the club would tackle prospective employers while for its part the club was not wholly aware of Alan's problem. It was an example which, once it became known, reminded others of the value of keeping in touch with Blackie and Russell –the men who could help provided they knew *all* the story. Initiative from pigs in difficulty was especially necessary because Blackie was heavily occupied with his multiplicity of tasks and Russell was still 'passing them out'.

In the event and fortunately Alan Morgan's story ended happily – far more happily than that of his hospital friend, Jock Duncan. A natural resilience which had helped him through so much adversity returned and he recovered magnificently once he had joined a company where managerial relations with the factory floor were superb.

* * *

If ever a member of aircrew could have allowed his disability to excuse him from further exposure to the perils of wartime flying it was Alan Morgan, but he was not alone among guinea pigs in battling to pass muster for 'another bash'.

Geoff Page, Frankie Truhlar, and a Canadian, Gordon Fredericks, number among guinea pigs who were repaired, went back to war, and then returned to the Sty for more. Richard Hillary's tragic story is too familiar to be repeated here, save that he wrote a letter shortly before he was killed on a night-flying course which revealed something of his state of mind when he returned to flying. The letter was written to Miss Wagg, sister of Alfred Wagg, first treasurer of the club, from the officers' mess, RAF Station, Charter Hall, near Duns in Berwickshire. It said:

> "Dear Miss Wagg, I am here for three months 'hard', learning to be a night fighter. When I say 'hard' I mean it, not only the camp which is understandable, but also the effort of re-orientating oneself to two years ago. Still, I'm glad I've made the decision. I'm happier for it – as long as I can do the job. I'm finding this night stuff devilishly difficult."

Throughout the war the maestro found himself under heavier pressure than he would have wished from guinea pigs whose optimism paid little respect to their wounds. Among the most persistent was Pilot Officer William Dewar, of whom McIndoe informed a medical board: "I have done no further work on this patient as he is very anxious to get back into action."

When a German cannon shell shattered Dewar's fighter cockpit over northern Europe in 1942, the thumb fell away from his right hand and he received many other injuries and lost most of the sight in his left eye. That thumb was the second right-handed thumb in his life. It was a dummy thumb and had been fitted by McIndoe in the course of earlier surgery so that he could continue to control a fighter aircraft.

By March 1943, Dewar had healed well and wore yet another new thumb, but his left eye was almost useless. The maestro's memorandum continued: "By the way, I would welcome some lead from you as to the disposal of one-eyed aircrew. I have a considerable number of them in my hands at the moment, all of whom are nagging away about flying. I would like, for instance your views on (a) one-eyed pilots, (b) one-eyed radio-operators, (c) one-eyed air-gunners. However, I thoroughly recommend this one-eyed pilot to you." After a letter like that he could truthfully tell his guinea pigs he was doing his best. There was in fact one one-eyed guinea pig who flew several times before the other eye's absence was discovered!

Here it should be made plain that McIndoe's collaboration with patients anxious to return to operational service was not activated solely by a desire to please them. There were other factors. Firstly, early in the war, while there was a shortage of operationally trained and experienced airmen, it was his duty. Secondly, some guinea pigs – badly fried though they may have been – were sound in hands and feet, boisterously fit between surgical operations, fit enough to fight again. Thirdly, and this is the consideration which was of the most vital importance to the future welfare of members of the Guinea Pig Club, there were patients who patently would never fly again and would provide easy fodder for the invaliding boards.

The more aircrew McIndoe could return to squadron service the better the case he built for the long term treatment scheme which he plugged and plugged to save guinea pigs from losing their Service status, uniform, pay, and prospects and enabled some to receive promotion at the Sty.

The long term treatment scheme was, therefore, perhaps the most important guinea pig concession wrung from Whitehall. McIndoe had been appalled by the official attitude that the sooner men whose hospital care was likely to exceed six months were invalided and pensioned, the tidier and the cheaper it would be.

Towards the end of the war when, following the personal intervention of Portal, Chief of the Air Staff, the long term scheme was working well and when trained operational aircrew were in fuller supply, the rate of repair and return to the battle began to decrease. It was a slowing-up process which was partly influenced by the state of the war, and partly by knowledge gained at the Sty, that some patients would appear to be able to tolerate only so many operations in a certain period and would then require a rest.

By the beginning of 1945, the year of victories in Europe and the Far East, even the spirit of guinea piggery was losing a little of its impetus. People everywhere were beginning to think about 'after the war'. This attitude invaded the Sty and the maestro began to recommend, as for James Sandeman-Allen: "His treatment is now completed, but I do think that this young man has had enough and hope that you will agree with me that he should be invalided out of the Service."

Nobody could dispute the assessment. Sandy had been concussed in two serious crashes, wounded fighting over Singapore, and shattered by a shell which entered the cockpit of his Typhoon over France. Nor could anyone have foreseen the beneficial impact Sandy would eventually have on the welfare of the club and its members when as treasurer he built a sound financial base and, following the chief guinea pig Tom Gleave's death in 1994, consolidated his years of administrative leadership as honorary chief executive. More later of Sandy's exploits in war and successful peacetime career as a chartered accountant.

As with his blunt request for Sandy's release McIndoe's note in 1944 to a medical board about another guinea pig was characteristically frank: "This flying officer was badly burned over Berlin and the machine was brought home with very great difficulty, the result being the survivors of the crew were all decorated. Unfortunately the boy went absolutely cold on flying and remained so during his whole period in hospital. He has twenty-five operational flights to his credit, but has really developed the jitters."

CHAPTER SIX

"You may not yourself have bought it badly, but there are many who have and it is for these less fortunate guinea pigs whose will to live is as strong as ever that this club really exists."

The original Reg Hyde, the young Reg Hyde who, before Germany invaded Poland went from Poole Grammar School into local government accountancy, ends where the strong-growing dark and curly hair meets the new Reg Hyde along the plimsoll line of his plastic surgery, high on the forehead. The old Reg begins again somewhere beneath the new chin which Jerry Moore suggested in the course of the bomber navigator's seventy major surgical operations.

His nose, his eyelids, his face, and much of his neck have been re-fashioned from skin grafted, or raised by pedicles, from the few parts of his body which escaped the flames when both engines of the Wellington bomber, in which he was instructing, cut. Sergeant George Lamb who lost his life in the fire, put her nose down and crash-landed the aircraft, known affectionately as the Wimpy after J. Wellington Wimpy, the Popeye cartoon character.

Reg's hands were badly burned too and inspection of the buckled fingers which proffered a tankard or turned the steering-wheel of his car, or helped his wife Jean pod the peas grown in their Crawley garden, magnified the marvel of the will with which Reg, ten years behind his ex-Service competitors for jobs, re-settled himself in civilian life. He qualified as a municipal engineer, passing his exams with but one concession gained on his behalf by the Guinea Pig Club – extra time to complete his papers because of the difficulty he experienced in writing and drawing.

Reg Hyde wore a blue blazer on weekends and on the

pocket the badge of No. 49 Squadron, the Lancaster
bomber squadron with which he had completed a tour of
operations over Germany before being rested with an
operational training unit as an instructor.

On the night of Reg's last flight the Wellington was
returning to Silverstone from a cross-country training flight
for a pupil crew of five with three instructors. Reg had put
away his navigation instruments and was waiting for
touch-down, thinking, "Well, there's another night's work
finished." He stood up with his head in the Wimpy's
distinctive astrodome to take a look round as the pilot
made his approach. George Lamb, he thought, was making
some comment over the intercom about the state of the
starboard engine, but Reg paid little attention to this as
there had been heavy static throughout the trip, and
straining to listen to exchanges on the intercom had grown
tiresome. Anyway, the flight was almost over.

Then, something happened which made Reg move very,
very fast in the confined navigator's area. The port engine
threw out a shower of sparks – and stopped. "This", Reg
recalled "was where drill comes in. Automatically I
thought – 'crash-landing positions' and I took mine up by
the main spar, feet up, facing the rear, and bracing myself
with my arms."

"We were over the runway and I thought if we're lucky
we'll get a jolt and everything will be ok." But the trouble
had developed at a critical moment. Another aircraft was
on the runway and normally Reg's pilot would have
increased power and made a fresh circuit. With the port
engine gone and the starboard engine ropey, this was
impossible. "The only action the pilot could take was to put
the nose down, overshoot the runway and attempt a crash
belly landing. This he did, passing over the other aircraft
which had landed safely, and in which Reg would have
been instructing that very night had he not made a friendly
swap in order to let another navigator, Eddie Warmington,
take the ride because he had been previously crewed up
with the pilot earlier in the war at Malta.

Many guinea pigs might have stood a chance of being
less severely burned had they been wearing gloves or
helmets and Archie McIndoe invariably asked them why
they had not worn the protection provided by kit issued to

them. Reg Hyde, who with Paul Hart and Godfrey Edmonds, numbered among the more disfigured members of the club, said: "One never thought about catching fire. It seemed very remote. I never wore gloves as a navigator because I couldn't do navigational work in them and they weren't necessary in heated cabins, and I had whipped off my helmet thinking of the danger of getting trapped by an intercom lead tangled in the wreckage."

Thus Reg braced himself in his crash position, gloves off, helmet off and not contemplating the possibility of fire. But the Wellington's wings slapped into two trees and, as Reg described it, he found himself "in the middle of a blazing bonfire". Before taking up his crash position Reg had tried to loosen the four bolts which held the astrodome, realising that almost certainly this would be his sole escape. He had loosened two bolts before the crash but after the impact he found that the astrodome had jammed. Struggling, he found himself growing more and more feeble. "I thought I'd just about had it when the dome moved and then the most extraordinary thing happened. One sometimes hears of people who discover superhuman strength in a moment of crisis. I would have found it difficult enough to escape through that hole in my fittest condition and yet I shot through there like a PT instructor, although I had to pull myself up through a hole which was shoulder high."

The fire was so intense that Reg could not see. He jumped on to the stub of one of the wings, both of which had been torn off by the trees and found himself up to the knees in the Barnes Wallis latticework geodetic design which was the outstanding feature of the Wellington bomber.

The wing, like the rest of the aircraft, was well alight. He picked himself out of the wing and gave a shout. "There was no reply, and after the roaring flames the silence seemed uncanny", Reg recalled. "I knew I had to get away from the wreck before it blew up. I climbed through a barbed-wire fence and over a ditch. It seemed so quiet. Just the steady crackling of the bomber and sheep bleating in the field." Reg learned later that there had been one other survivor. Upon impact, the rear-gunner was thrown clear and knocked unconscious. He was soon mended. He had only broken an ankle.

Reg believed that at the outset ignorance about burns and their long and painful treatment saved many guinea pigs much mental torture:

"I realised of course I had been burned but I thought about burns in terms of scalding a hand with a boiling kettle, or of an accident with a hot iron, or even with a candle. When the ambulance delivered me at the RAF Hospital, Halton, in October 1943, I thought 'I'll stay here long enough to get some good Christmas leave and then the treatment will be all over.' I stayed there until May the next year and even then because the fire had burned away all the muscles I could hardly open my mouth, I had to be fed and to drink through a rubber tube."

When McIndoe, making one of his rounds of hospitals his guinea pigs called 'the burneries' – the RAF hospitals with burns units – suggested Reg's transfer to East Grinstead, Reg was pleased to leave. "You get a bit hospital-bound and need a change of scene. Moreover, there had been a recent hospital film show which featured the story of a beautiful girl who had suffered terrible facial injuries in a car crash and in the film she was made as beautiful as ever by plastic surgery. This gave me a lot of hope – false hope as it turned out – but it made me very keen to get to East Grinstead."

By this time Reg's morale was very low. Far from being out of hospital by Christmas, it was now the beginning of the next summer and still he could not eat or drink. At the Sty they understood the importance of a patient's state of mind and when Jerry Moore said: "We'll do your mouth so that you can eat", the surgeon knew that the hope of being able to eat and drink with other guinea pigs would raise Reg Hyde's spirits. For, without a mouth to control his food and drink, Reg had to lie flat on his back to take in any nourishment. Even so, three more years were to pass before Reg could drink without a rubber tube.

Jean and Reg Hyde produced three handsome children, Susan, John and Peter. In Crawley neighbours and friends congratulated Jean on the good looks and clear skin of the children and when this occurred Jean knew that behind the remark there were two unspoken questions – how can such a disfigured man be the father of such fine children, and was it right to take the risk of having them? It is only later, of course, when such well-intentioned people have stopped to think that they have realised that Reg's disfigurement was not congenital and that he could not possibly pass it on.

The RAF had issued Reg with an escape photograph of himself for use on forged identity papers in the event of coming down over Europe and attempting to evade capture. For the rest of his life it remained Reg's link with his former identity and because he was still the same man within it was how he felt himself to be. But comparison of the new and the old Reg makes the error of Jean's unthinking acquaintances understandable.

Jean said she never noticed the disfigurement of any of the guinea pigs but she admitted this was not always so. She had taken a course in tropical nursing at the Hospital for Tropical Diseases before applying for a nursing post at East Grinstead. "I thought I'd seen some pretty gruesome looking patients among the returned Japanese prisoners-of-war", she said. "I knew very little about the work at East Grinstead, but I was intrigued when I applied for the post that I was asked to send a photograph. It seemed an odd way to select nursing staff for a hospital.

"'I was even more surprised when I arrived because on my third day two French airmen asked me to a cocktail party in the ward, and I thought 'what a queer hospital'. The first time I went to an operating theatre, Jock Duncan was on the slab and I thought, 'Frankenstein has nothing on this!'"

Reg Hyde, like so many guinea pigs, was transferred from an RAF burnery to East Grinstead at the maestro's personal request though not every serviceman with the requisite wounds was fortunate enough to be rescued from the harsher realities of RAF or other military hospitals.

It was a sad fact of red tape and service hospital starch that the bright and breezy, free and easy reputation at East Grinstead should have presented such a remarkable haven to the badly injured men who so gratefully were transferred there. Sam Gallop still remembers with horror the rigid discipline of an RAF hospital where it seemed

ludicrous, as a legless man, to be commanded to lie to
attention when there was so little of him left. No legs to
stiffen as the parade ground bellow filled the ward. Not
even a jaw to broaden a grin at such nonsense. Like Sam's
legs, most of it had gone.

Sam's schoolboy son Nicholas played his part in carrying
forward the Gallop desire to perpetuate the spirit of guinea
piggery. He initiated a Squeakers Page in *Guinea Pig*, the
club's magazine. "Our club", he wrote in his first issue, "is
called the Squeakers Club because a young guinea pig
squeaks and because our fathers are guinea pigs."

* * *

Some patients, attracted by stories of wards awash with
beer, wangled their way to East Grinstead, as had
Smith-Barry, using Phillipi to persuade McIndoe to accept
him. A few gained entry through the influence of guinea
pigs encountered in base. A Fleet Air Arm pilot who
bemoaned his fate to Jimmy Wright over a pint obtained
admission after tenderly delivering one blind, if not blind
drunk DFC to the Sty.

Andre Browne, who after two operational tours as a
fighter pilot had crashed in a twin-engine aircraft with
which as a single-engine pilot he was unfamiliar, owed his
admission to a Canadian. Having heard of the new
Canadian wing at the Queen Victoria Hospital the
Canadian pleaded to be sent there so that he might be
operated upon by his compatriot, RCAF surgeon Ross
Tilley. Listening, ears-cocked in the next bed, Andre
suggested that it might do his morale good if he
accompanied the Canadian "just for the fresh air and the
trip". As the Canadian was being tucked up in his new bed
at the Sty, and Andre was saying goodbye, the maestro
walked into the ward. "You can stay too", he said. Andre
Browne was delighted, although in the middle of that night
he wondered whether he had made a mistake. The bed of a
badly burned Canadian caught fire.

In truth, Andre was little fazed because he was already
no stranger to surprise in East Grinstead. Some while
before he became a guinea pig he had been sent for a
week's recuperation at Dutton Homestall, a country house

which the Dewar whiskey family had provided for resting officers, and his life was almost certainly saved by an astonishing piece of luck. It was customary for a celebrity to attend Sunday lunch and give a short address after the meal. On this occasion Andre, who had arranged to get to East Grinstead's Whitehall Cinema in time for the afternoon house, was vexed when Hannen Swaffer, the *People* Sunday newspaper's columnist, was still speaking after an hour. Much delayed and on his way to the cinema, Andre was stopped by a shocked policeman who told him the cinema had just been bombed with appalling casualties.

Some guinea pigs, like Sam Gallop, were broken and crunched, not fried, and the grogging club's first title, the Maxillonians, gives the clue to why some of them were admitted to the Queen Victoria Hospital. The maxilio-facial unit was equipped to mend smashed faces and the records of some guinea pigs contain the ugly description 'dishfaced'. John Kirby was thus typecast after one engine cut during a night take-off in a twin-engine trainer and, failing to climb into the darkness above blacked-out Britain, he went smack into a concrete pill-box and began his career as a guinea pig.

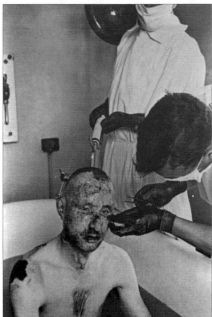

Top: The Queen Victoria Hospital, Main Building, circa 1943.

Bottom left: The state of burned airmen when rescued from the sea gave the clue to saline bath treatment for burns.

Middle right: A typical East Grinstead group during wartime.

Bottom right: The saline bath, 1942.

Top: Ward 3, birthplace of the Guinea Pig Club, Christmas 1941.

Above left: Sister Meally, legendary Ward 3 victim of guinea pig pranks.

Above right: Miss Caroline Hall, former Matron at the Hospital.

Right: Marchwood Park provided respite from the Sty and round the clock partying. In one memorable rag Blackie was debagged.

Bottom left: Away from the 'slab' Archie McIndoe hosted and attended numerous functions on behalf of his guinea pigs.

Bottom right: The maestro Archie McIndoe (at piano) entertains the guinea pigs. From left to right; Bill Gardner, Sam Gallop, Jimmy Wright, George Hindley, Pip Parratt, Bill Warman, Noel 'Doc' Newman, Jack Allaway, Jock Morris, Eric Brunskill, Ray Brooke and Tommy Brandon.

Top: Connie McIndoe poses with her husband, Archie McIndoe (left) and Edward 'Blackie' Blacksell.

Top: Canadian guinea pigs at the opening of the Ross Tilley Public School, 5 November 1996.

Bottom left: The 'Wingco' Ross Tilley, who commanded the Canadian Wing, with Marjorie Jackson, his Chief Assistant, and 'Ulysses'.

Bottom right: Hank and Mary Hastings over from Canada for the fiftieth anniversary. Hank became a dentist.

Top: Tubby Taylor (left), and Jock Tosh entertaining at a lost weekend poolside party.

Above: No lost weekend is complete without a pint at The Guinea Pig pub where Jack Toper (fourth from left) holds court.

Right: Archie at the site of many lost weekend frolics, The Guinea Pig pub.

Top: Jimmy Wright in uniform, before he was grievously injured and blinded.

Bottom: Jimmy parascending the Channel for charity.

Top: March 1986. Jimmy Wright, sightless guinea pig who built a film business, and Moira Stewart meet Princess Diana at a Hammersmith Palais function.

Bottom: Julie Andrews is escorted by Jimmy Wright at a fundraising event.

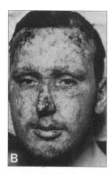

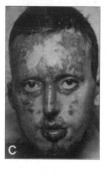
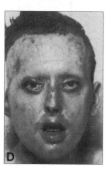
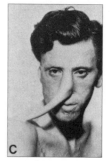

Top left: Between them Jack Toper (left) and Jack Allaway have rendered many years of service to their fellow guinea pigs as editor of the magazine and welfare organiser.

Top right: Jack Toper (centre) and Sandy Sandeman-Allen (centre right) meet the president HRH Prince Philip at an anniversary dinner.

Bottom: Stages of the reconstruction of Jack Allaway's face. McIndoe was

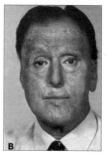

always particularly pleased with the results of the surgery.

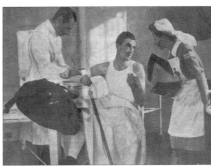

Top left: Sandy Sandeman-Allen survived perilous combat encounters in the Far East before Typhoon exploits over France. He is pictured by the tail of his shot up Typhoon.

Top right: Czech guinea pig Alois Siska, who flew Wellington bombers, is welcomed by Ann Standen at a lost weekend she helped to organise in 1997.

Middle left: Sandy Sandeman-Allen features in the *Sunday Pictorial*, Oct 10, 1943.

Bottom: While Sandy masterminds the annual reunion, Joan has the interests of wives at heart.

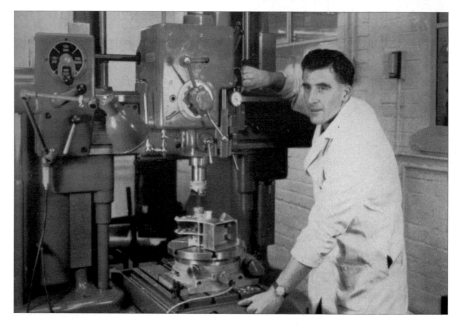

Top left: This sketch of Tom Gleave was drawn by Archie McIndoe's brother John at the the Whitehall Restaurant on 25th July, 1945.

Top right: Chief guinea pig Tom Gleave receiving the C.P. Robertson Trophy from Chief of the Air Staff ACM Sir Keith Williamson, GCB, AFC, in May 1983.

Middle right: Ella and Alan Morgan. Attempts to save Alan's fingers failed.

Bottom: Despite losing his fingers to frostbite, Alan Morgan worked as a jig borer working to a fraction of an inch.

Top left: Jim Verran in uniform (right), before he was shot down over Denmark.

Top right: Jim Verran in silhouette by Mike Pierce which appeared in the book *For So Many*, published by the RAF Benevolent Fund to honour Bomber Command aircrew.

Bottom: After the war, New Zealand-born Jim Verran followed a career in civil aviation.

Top: Sgt Jack Mann's birth as a guinea pig, photographed by himself after he escaped his burning Spitfire.

Middle left: Captain Jack Mann (left) at the controls of a Middle East Airlines Comet, twenty-one years after his Spitfire crashed.

Bottom left: Eileen and Dickie Richardson, who became a switchboard operator, with their twins, Heather and Keith.

Bottom right: Sgt Dickie Richardson lost his sight and right hand after his Lancaster bomber burst into flames over France.

Top: Reg Hyde became a fully qualified municipal engineer.

Middle, left and right: Sid McQuillan, and the burnt-nose of the aircraft from which he emerged to become a guinea pig.

Right: Reg Hyde, very badly burned in a Wellington bomber, had more than seventy surgical operations.

Top: Eric Lock obtained most of his twenty-six 'kills' after becoming a guinea pig.

Right: The Guinea Pig Club logo was painted on one of the Spitfires (AB910) belonging to the Battle of Britain Memorial Flight. The letters EB:J were also added, these being the identification letters of George Bennions' and Eric Lock's squadron.

Top left: Fairey Battle survivor Bill Simpson takes a turn with his wife Myrtle when guinea pigs visited Prague.

Top right: Reunited in Prague, from left to right; Bill Simpson, Bill Foxley, Alois Siska and Jack Allaway.

Middle: Sir Roger Palin (left), former Controller of the RAF Benevolent Fund, draws the raffle at a guinea pig lost weekend.

Right: Bill Simpson in uniform.

Top left: Les Wilkins, Lady 'Barnsie' Sassoon and Tubby Taylor at a lost weekend party.

Top right: Lady Connie McIndoe and Max Bygraves at a guinea pig dance, 1962, to celebrate twenty-one years of the Guinea Pig Club.

Middle left: Sam Gallop and his wife Ré were honoured by the Duke of Edinburgh's attendance at a lunch in 1983 to celebrate Sam's OBE.

Bottom: Her Majesty Queen Elizabeth, Patron of the Queen Victoria Hospital, at the entrance of the Cottage Hospital where she opened the American Wing, July 25th, 1946. Front row, from left to right; Archie McIndoe, Guthrie Kirkhope, Lady Kindersley, HM The Queen, Matron Hall and Sir William Kelsey Fry.

CHAPTER SEVEN

"It has always been my belief that whenever he could a guinea pig should fall into a woman's arms but not into her hands."

Only men can be admitted into membership of the Guinea Pig Club, but the Sty was not, of course, an all-male world and it would be unchivalrous to carry the club's story further without recalling the devotion of Matron Hall and her nurses, many of whom, in company with Sister Meally of Ward 3, married guinea pigs.

It is a very exceptional woman who will accept prolonged disturbance of her settled and preferred routine. Consider then the nightmare situation of Matron Hall when war brought an unruly invasion of her tidy little cottage hospital at East Grinstead, led by a surgeon who rolled barrels of beer into her wards and whom patients and staff called the boss or the maestro.

Guinea pigs, wheresoever they dispersed after the war, were hugely indebted for far more than magnificent nursing to Matron Hall and Sister Cherry Hall, her sister, who were both eventually to retire to their native Ireland. Without their co-operation and through them the dedicated work of the Queen Victoria Hospital's pre-war and wartime nursing staff, the Guinea Pig Club would never have grown and flourished. Only a matron in a million would have permitted her hospital to become a hotel where her night sisters acted like night porters to let in the revellers and set up the nightcaps and sandwiches as though her wards were a club house with a twenty-four hour licence.

Jimmy Wright and Flash McConnell, returning from a London night club, walked into the ward at five a.m. one morning as the night sister who, had only been at the hospital for a few days, was doing her last round. "Oh you are up early, are you going somewhere?" she asked innocently.

Andre Browne remembered that on one occasion the ragging became so violent that, in his opinion, some guinea pigs went too far and a nurse would leave a bedside in floods of tears. "But", Andre said, "the maestro would walk in and take the side of the guinea pig."

"These men have put up with a hell of a lot and so you can put up with just a little nonsense", he told nurses who complained.

A fragment written shortly after the Battle of Britain by a fighter pilot who did not identify himself – it was lodged loosely among some pensions correspondence of Russell Davies – gives a clue to Matron Hall's remarkable talent for encouraging just the right balance of behaviour between her staff and the guinea pigs, and to her patience and understanding.

The burned pilot had noted that he had returned to the hospital two days overdue "to undergo the first of a long series of operations to make my face and hands a more presentable picture. The matron greeted me and I hastily explained to her that the air raids in London were the cause of my being two days late. An amused twinkle came into her eyes. It was quite obvious she knew that I had spent the last two days painting London a dark shade of red." In *The Last Enemy* Richard Hillary has left a similar impression of Matron Hall's hospital and her staff who made no distinction between the Battle of Britain pilots and their less polished Bomber Command successors, the Henry Standens, the Jack Topers, the George Hindleys and the Alan Morgans of the Guinea Pig Club.

Hailing from back streets, clerks' stools, the drapers' shops, grammar and council schools to replenish the bomber crews as losses mounted over Berlin, Hamburg, Essen, Dusseldorf, Frankfurt – and other places airline pilots will take you to today – these guinea pigs formed the core of the club. They were the guinea pigs the maestro had in mind when he declared: "As we worked a persistent question nagged at my mind: When their bodies are whole again can we also rebuild something of their lives?"

John Kirby was one of these men. He was not so well educated and sophisticated as some of the Battle of Britain patients in Ward 3, but he could *feel* and what he felt he described. His picture of the Sty reflects, unintentionally, the nightmare faced by Matron Hall and how she and her nurses maintained hospital efficiency throughout all the high jinks.

He wrote:

"I was not fried and as a result I was shunted into Ward 1. I had never been a patient in a hospital before although I had been a visitor on several occasions. When I looked round Ward 1 I began to wonder. I must say that, except for the beds with bods in various stages of repair, I thought that it would make a good barrack block or storehouse. The beds were forces' issue. Low black things with spring mattresses. Strangely enough I was not upset by this impression. There just seemed to be an atmosphere of efficiency.

"After the hospital beds of Innsworth [RAF hospital] I felt that I was much too near the floor. Doctors and nurses seemed to be looking down from a great height. I arrived at midday. The next morning someone came and pushed something like clay in my mouth. What the hell was going on? I soon found out. A set of splints were cemented to my jaws, both upper and lower. A carpenter came down the ward with long pieces of two-by-two and started to erect a scaffold over my bed.

"Up to this point I had no idea what was going on. I was so bemused. . . .These splints are giving me hell. They are not only encasing my teeth but also parts of my gums. A post is erected at the head of the bed and another at the foot with a connecting piece across the top. No fuss. No bother. Just Heath Robinson [designer of outrageous contraptions] sort of material. The scaffold is ready. Where's the hangman?

"Here he comes. Funny he isn't wearing a mask. He has a round, kindly face and gives the impression that he knows what he is going to do. I remember I had seen him before when I first came into this hospital. Round face [it was McIndoe] was talking to his assistant about 'middle third borkum beam', or that's what it sounded like. All double Dutch to me. Two pulleys were put on the cross beam and the boss and his assistant – a Brown job [Army] named Captain Sheffield – produced a piece of cord. This was attached to the hook on the top set of splints over the pulleys and lo and behold bags of shot, or the like, were tied to the end. After another inspection the chief and his assistant left me.

"Here come the nurses and I think it must be sister with them. Slim, unsmiling, severe. Oh so severe. 'Take that pillow away.' Glory be! She's Irish. When everything was shipshape they left me. I wish I knew what was going on. They had left me strung up like a stuck pig. My bloody ribs are aching like hell but I can't turn over. This damned cord keeps me flat out on my back. I suddenly realised that I have only one useful eye. The right eye doesn't seem to be open. It doesn't seem to matter.

"I remember vaguely seeing my wife when I was at Innsworth. Where is she now? After a few days my wife came in to see me and I was shocked. I have read novels in which the author describes a person's eyes as 'dead'. I suddenly realised what they were trying to convey. My wife's eyes had no expression. They were 'dead'. Yes, I was beginning to notice things, even with only one eye.

"Sister Harrington was still the same severe person. Everything must be just so. I wonder where she was trained. After about a fortnight I was beginning to waken up. Groups of RAF, Army, and Navy officers would occasionally gather round my bed and someone would give them a lecture. In this way I began to piece together what had happened and also what was being done to straighten me out.

"The upper jaw was gradually responding to the pressure of the weights and was coming out. Eventually the constant pressure pulled the jaw out but even now only two teeth meet. There was a gap of something like one eighth inch between my front teeth. Strong elastic was put onto hooks and down, oh so slowly, came the top set. The day came when my front teeth overlapped. The elastics came off and on went some wire fixed by a pair of pliers.

"Now I can get rid of these weights. These ribs have given me hell. After my mechanic has finished I ask the captain to take off the cord. He walked to the end of the bed, lifted the weights, stood for about ten seconds, put the weights back again, then came and asked me if I had felt any pain. I'll say I had. It seems that the top jaw was trying to go back and I had, during those few seconds, a terrific pain just in front of my ears. No, it was going to be a gradual process.

"There is a Doctor Jayes keeps coming round and one day he sprang a surprise. [This was Mr Percy Jayes, the plastic surgeon, who later sprang another surprise on the guinea pigs by marrying the 'severe' Sister Harrington.] 'Do you drink beer or stout?' Can a duck swim! When the shock wore off I found that I was to have half a pint of beer every day. Taffy [fellow patient] and I shared a pint to the envious glances of the rest of the boys. Now that I was beginning to take stock I saw the aforementioned Taffy walking about with a tube from his face into his dressing gown. Jacky across the ward was taken down into the block at regular intervals. One day's peace. Then he was back to his usual chatty self.

"There is a wind rushing down the ward but I cannot see what is going on. The movement is working up the ward. Now I see the old beds are being replaced by pukka hospital beds. All, that is, with one exception. Mine!

"I still have my scaffold. My bed spoils the new look. The fellow in the next bed is beginning to revive and leans over to have a chat. We begin to get to know each other. John Bubb had returned from his first op with a broken jaw and smashed leg. Something about bullets in his turret.

"Lying there with only a limited field of vision, mainly the roof, I had plenty of time to think and listen. I recall that at Innsworth I was given the usual hospital rations. A square of cheese, a piece of marge, a piece of bread. I didn't eat any of the food. I couldn't. My wife used to bring custards and a sloppy food supplied by the kindly person who gave her a bed near the hospital.At this place I am on what they call jaw food. I am not the only one on this slop. There must be several of the boys in the same boat, judging by the number of feeding mugs that are on the tray.

"I am surprised at the way the hospital is run. Some of the fellows who are able to get out don't always come back after tea. After about 7.30 p.m. everybody seems to settle and all is peace and quiet until 10, 11 and even 12 p.m. Then I hear the sounds of the return of the merrymakers. I must still be delirious. That fellow is drunk. It would never happen in hospital. You can see I was still a new boy.

"The great day arrives. The man everyone referred to as Mac, the boss, gave permission for the cord to be taken off. Glory be! I can turn on my side. All these weeks I have had to lie flat on my back whilst someone came and made my bed, gave me a bed bath, took the dressings off my hands, picked off the scabs, messed about with the cuts on my face. There was a nurse seemed to be an expert at these picking operations.

"Now I can turn and see my neighbours but even now I can't see right down the ward. I am still in the low bed. The next day I get the new bed. The ward is now completely re-equipped. I remember the pleased expressions on the faces of the doctors and sisters. Even Sister Harrington smiled and nodded with satisfaction and somehow I felt better. I had been the blot on the landscape, holding back the improvement and smartness. Now I was not a drawback. Don't misunderstand. No one had by glance, remark or in any way suggested that I was the odd man out. I just know.

"I now had visions of sitting up, let alone having a pillow but all that was squashed by sister. 'You can have one pillow', she said it in the same tone that I imagine Scrooge would use when giving away a crust. Although she was so unbending I had developed a great feeling of confidence in our sister. She knew just what I could be allowed to do and although I sometimes tried to persuade her to let me sit up I was now prepared to accept her word. I'm afraid I pulled her leg, or rather I tried. She seemed so unbending. Two pillows then I was allowed as back rest just for a few minutes so that I could shave.

"The bloody ward is on a turntable. I can't keep my face in the mirror. I'm damned well not going to get down until I have shaved. At last I have had a scrape. What a relief to lie down again but don't let sister know. She may not let me have it tomorrow. I didn't fool her for one minute.

"Here comes Robby with his plaster jacket and arm in the air. Last night he was allowed out to a dance. He and Jacky took my wife. They were both stinking when they came back and Robby lay on his bed incapable except for his voice. He proceeded to give a performance of barrack room songs. The nurses on night stint got these two undressed and put them to bed.

"I have never ceased to admire those girls, most of them VADs [Voluntary Aid Detachment] coping with situations like that. The next time the boys went out they again took Ginger and the wife, and at about midnight there was a knock at the window against my bed. I opened it and took in the four bottles of 'milk' (beer). This milk run became a regular operation and John Bubb and I used to have our own celebrations.

"There was a sailor on the opposite side of the ward. His mouth was always watering when I had my half pint ration. He got himself organised and had his regular supply of medicine.

"I had to laugh at his description of his first trip out. He was taken out in a chair which had pockets at the side and back. When the chair left the hospital it was loaded with empty bottles. When they got on to the drive there was such a rattling and clanking of bottles that they had to sing loud and long to hide the sound. Half way down the drive they met the boss . . .

"Came the day when the plaster is taken off my ankle. This is painful. The plaster is stuck to the hairs on my leg. Oh don't pull. It's surprising how comparatively small things seem much more painful. I was still one-eyed. My right eye is still closed but I am still cocky. I tell the doctors that I know that I shall get better and that I shall go back flying. They shake their heads. Time goes by and I am allowed to get up. I am shocked when I am allowed to take my first bath. My legs are only about the same thickness as my arms. Gradually I improve and then I am told I can go into East Grinstead. Not alone. I must have a chaperone. My right eye is now open but the sight has not yet returned. I realize that everything is not quite as it should be. My guide saves me when I try to step down a double curb with one step. I'll have to go carefully.

"My teeth are freed from the wire and Mr Ridley, the eye specialist, invites me to a Rotary Club Lunch. The main course was fish. I remember how awkward I was with my knife and fork. My first night out. A Red Cross dance. Everyone is so kind. The people of East Grinstead are the most kindly and understanding people I know. There is one person I shall always remember, the late Mrs Fraser. A most charming person in every way.

"My stay at EG was filled with incidents. Like the night we got back to the annexe at 1 a.m. We tried the windows. None would open. Matron greeted us from the front entrance, inviting us to enter by the door."

The guinea pigs' relationship with Matron Hall and their debt to her and her nursing staff is implicit in John Kirby's simple, telling narrative. It may be surprising, therefore, that while privileged with the status of 'friends' they were never admitted to the Guinea Pig Club.

McIndoe had wished to open membership to them and at the annual meeting of the club in 1945 he sought a precedent by prevailing upon Flight Lieutenant Harold Stannus, an Australian guinea pig, to move the immediate election of Sister Jill Mullins, his theatre assistant and of Sister Meally of Ward 3. McIndoe supported the motion from the chair but it suffered a heavy defeat. George Taylor, also from Australia, recalled: "The boss accepted the decision with good grace and a democratic spirit, but it was the only time I can recollect a failure by him to sway a body of pigs to his way of thinking.

"Probably there was not one person in the room who did not want each of those two wonderful girls to be one of us, but it was felt that the Guinea Pig Club was a men's club and ladies should join the pigs as guests. Further, there were others to be considered – Matron Hall, Sisters Cherry Hall, Harrington, Polly Walker and Mary Rae."

Some guinea pigs found themselves falling in love with their nurses as quickly as it took them to slip a thermometer into a mangled mouth and occasionally their visitors and supporters followed suit. Sir Victor Sassoon, who paid for one of the club's annual dinners out of his horse St Paddy's Derby winnings and whose widow, Barnsie, endowed the club with some of St Paddy's subsequent stud fees, married *his* nurse, a great supporter and favourite at reunions.

The patient-nurse marriage rate at the Sty was high. Many of the nurses, some possibly motivated by compassion, married guinea pigs, ensuring that Britain, the Commonwealth and even eastern Europe were satisfactorily sprinkled with guinea piglets. Some guinea pigs rooted beyond the Sty for romance, finding love in some odd places. Gus Fowler, who had been a tea planter in Assam before the war, met his wife in a nudist camp.

Of course, guinea pig marriages have foundered, but not disproportionately to the usual pattern. Some of the club's most disabled members who remained bachelors were ribbed that this was because you can't leave home when your legs are locked up in a cupboard for the night and the wife sleeps with the key under her pillow.

But, to be serious, marriage for a guinea pig could be a minefield. McIndoe was reminded frequently that the ordinary pitfalls of marriage could become canyons for a guinea pig. Towards the end of the war and for some years afterwards the club's correspondence on the subject was heavy. Blackie, Russell and the boss were confronted with such cases as that of the guinea pig whose future wife was expecting before club-assisted divorce proceedings had started. Or of the member who wrote: "You may be able to recall our discussing my somewhat unhappy matrimonial problems when I was last at the hospital some two years ago having my left eye removed."

Occasionally, McIndoe unbent on the subject of guinea pigs and marriage but when he did his words presented a balanced blend of reproof, humour, practical advice, irony and humanitarian understanding. At the annual dinner in 1950, he said:

> "You will remember that the problems of guinea pigs during the five war years were really comparatively simple ones, though they involved big principles. These, I used crudely to say, concerned women, jobs and money. They were solved by methods well known to you.
>
> "The past five years have, however, brought to light many more complicated tangles in the field of human relations; the result of all the forces at work when you combine physical disability with marriage and with the struggle for survival in this anxious and uncertain world. When you ask us for help in this field we are often at our wits end to know what to say or do – whether to advise or remain silent.
>
> "It has always been my belief that, whenever he could, a guinea pig should fall into a woman's arms but not into her hands; that while it is important that, if possible, you should find and cleave to the one woman in the world who will make you supremely happy, it is much more important that you should avoid the thousands who can make your life supremely miserable. I do realise, of course, that this little bit of advice is somewhat late for you have mostly made your selections and are now reaping the benefits or the whirlwind.
>
> "It is somewhat disquieting to note, however, that domestic problems are on the increase and, while we have done what we can, we do not profess to be very proficient in delivering Solomonic judgements – where the wife has decided that the handsome Romeo down the street is more desirable than her slightly singed guinea pig, or on the contrary, where the slightly singed guinea pig has decided that if he can't get the plums out of a cake he will feel better if he kicks the missus. Tolerance and understanding between two people will do more in this field than third-party interference and I commend this course to those of you who stand in need of it."

Thus far would McIndoe go. He steered the Guinea Pig Club into many areas of self-help, including its thriving, string-pulling job finding operation. But there were two roles he was determined the club must not play. Those of marriage bureau and marriage guidance council. Though for the former there was certainly no call. In 1952 when he replied to an offer of a job for an *unmarried* guinea pig schoolmaster which had reached him from the little West Indian Island of St Vincent he wrote: "The trouble is those who have stayed single are certainly not in the field of education."

When in 1959 Jimmy Wright, who had lost his sight as an RAF combat cameraman, met Jan Jessey he had established himself in the film business and was living at Shepperton in Surrey near the studios where he made some of his films.

He was helping a fellow St Dunstaner who was confined to a wheelchair to enjoy a seaside respite at Lee-on-Solent in Hampshire when he met Jan. There was a whirlwind romance at the Marine Court hotel near the Tower ballroom, a dance hall with romantic wartime memories for men and women serving at *Daedalus*, the former Fleet Air Arm base.

Almost immediately Jimmy knew that he wanted to marry this lively girl who, as it happened, was secretary to an eye surgeon and sadly aware that Jimmy would never recover his sight. He swept Jan off to Paris, bought her a silk dress, and escorted her on a round of parties and events which remained central to guinea pig therapy. Jan enjoyed the whirlwind and *joie de vivre* which Jimmy brought to everything he did. She admired the drive and courage of this blind and disfigured man who had sustained some eighty surgical operations and a long period of St Dunstan's training to equip him to work in a medium normally presumed closed to a blind producer.

But admiration and sympathy does not necessarily lead to love and Jan was uncertain at this stage that she loved Jimmy. After two years she took the painful decision to withdraw from what she perceived as a one-sided romance. Although they did not associate for five years Jimmy wrote regularly, sending greetings and presents. For Jimmy it was a bleak period to which in their future happy years together they were always to refer as the 'Cold War'.

It did not thaw until 1967 when, phoning Jimmy to thank him for a present, Jan agreed to meet him at Lee-on-Solent where the Fleet Air Arm's celebrated Royal Tournament gun crew which trained at *Daedalus*, habitually hosted a party of St Dunstaners.

Since Jimmy had said he would never propose again Jan took the initiative and they married, producing two sons, Christopher who followed his father into the film world and Nicholas who became a scientist. But Jan soon realised that the duties of being a mother were a mere fraction of her responsibilities as wife to a busy, bustling husband who was never to permit blindness and a measure of physical disablement to deny his professional ambitions or charitable work for which he was appointed OBE. There were also a string of professional awards among which Jimmy's British Academy of Film and Television Arts (BAFTA) award in 1981 was perhaps the most cherished.

The award recognised a career in which, beginning with Anglo Scottish Films and leading to Film City and Cinexsa, Jimmy survived the vicissitudes of financing and producing documentaries and television commercials and poised himself for further success. His more recent *Avalanche*, a fifty minute ski training production was an international success and remains in demand. Jimmy, employing his film expertise, also joined fellow guinea pig Sam Gallop in some of his many endeavours on behalf of disabled people, not least *Disablement in the City* aimed at finding jobs for disabled people and *Employment Opportunities for People with Disabilities* offering nationwide assistance under the patronage of the Duke of Edinburgh, the Guinea Pig Club's president.

Spurred by Sam's drive and his particular talent for making organisations work, this body expanded from two small rooms in the Bank of England to a national service with twelve regional offices. Another of Jimmy's films, *Second Sight*, covered all aspects of teaching Braille to children whose eye conditions vary.

Jimmy remained dedicated to fundraising for those he considered even less fortunate than himself and in 1990, approaching seventy and seeking a way to benefit the RAF Benevolent Fund's Battle of Britain fiftieth anniversary appeal, he volunteered to parascend across the Channel.

Despite poor weather conditions, inadequate equipment and support at sea, Jimmy succeeded and raised £6,500 for the Fund. Locally, Jimmy was closely involved with Julie Andrews in fundraising to assist sufferers of arterial disease and before he died in 1993 aged seventy he launched Spelthorne Talking News which continues to bring recorded world, national and local news to blind people in the community.

Sam Gallop's collaboration with Jimmy Wright in support of his work on behalf of the disabled is a mere fraction of this grievously injured and legless guinea pig's past and continuing efforts over the past half century on behalf of his fellow guinea pigs for which, as with Jimmy, he has been appointed an OBE. He has never allowed the loss of his legs, third degree burns, spinal crush fracture, maxilio-facial injuries, broken arms and loss of a ring finger when piloting an Airspeed Oxford, to frustrate his career or charitable work.

After all that and equipped with four school A-levels he entered Brasenose College, Oxford and in 1949 graduated with an upper second in politics, philosophy and economics and was driving without hand controls. We have encountered him previously at the Central Electricity Generating Board from which in 1977 he retired as deputy secretary and chief management services officer.

Sam passed over the chance to ease up and seized the opportunity to devote much of his time to the Guinea Pig Club and the welfare of his fellow members. He also accepted trusteeships with the East Grinstead Medical Research Trust and Blond McIndoe Centre for Burns Research whose work continues to be so handsomely supported by the club. Among Sam's many and varied other activities chairmanship of the Limbless Association and of emPOWER, a consortium of thirty-six charities in the disablement field and publications concerning disablement and rehabilitation represent part of a very busy life as he reaches the age of eighty.

Perhaps the pace of Sam's life owes something to the fact that when all those years ago he sought to improve his own tin leg mobility by dancing, he could only manage the quickstep. Certainly, his lifelong record of combining a successful professional career with helping others owes much to the support of his wife Rénate – Ré – Trier, a refugee from Hitler's Germany, whom he met at Spanish evening classes in 1949 and married the next year.

Ré says: "I was very impressed because he had a car and a Parker pen." If these were rare possessions in postwar Britain so were Ré's views on marriage. She says: "I was rather old fashioned and a hausfrau instead of a career woman." Not expecting Sam to help with the chores Ré "left him with plenty of time to devote to work instead of washing up and doing the garden." In addition to Nicholas, last encountered as the magazine's Squeakers editor she also produced Suzanne and, with Sam, adopted Chris.

Jimmy, meeting Jan, had swept her off to a party. Nothing unusual about that because, though a solo enterprise, it was entirely in the spirit of guinea piggery. Lost weekends at East Grinstead continue to provide opportunities for a series of parties but down the years there have also been less attended if equally enjoyable get togethers – especially those arranged regularly by Les Syrett and Jack Perry, organiser of all manner of outings.

Les, who broke his back, neck, elbow, shoulder and crushed several internal organs when flight-testing a Manchester twin-engine bomber, returned to an insurance office after the war. Many of his clients were in the theatre. As a member and treasurer of the Green Room Club he had the ideal base and venue for arranging fun occasions for his fellow guinea pigs. When some years ago Jimmy Wright suggested that guinea pigs join the annual Remembrance Day parade and march past the Cenotaph in Whitehall Les organised lunch in the Green Room after the parade.

One of Jack Perry's many initiatives was to organise a Christmas lunch. When it outgrew its very limited venue Les suggested moving to the Farnell Arms, his local at Weybridge in Surrey and numbers increased to at least forty. Jack's chief event remains an annual day out at Harwell village and the Atomic Energy Research Establishment.

CHAPTER EIGHT

"We've had some mad Australians
Some French, some Czechs, some Poles,
We've even had some Yankees,
God bless their precious souls.
While as for the Canadians
Ah! That's a different thing
They couldn't stand our accent
And built a separate wing."
(Last verse of the Guinea Pig anthem.)

Blackie wrote the words of the Guinea Pig anthem. He said it was because he had become rather bored by the maudlin rendering of 'The Church's one Foundation' in the Old Brown Cow, the ramshackle bus which returned guinea pigs to the Sty from so many drinking excursions. The anthem has lasted but the mood in which it is sung annually at the dinner has changed since the Old Brown Cow's riotous journeys.

Like their author, Blackie, who remained eternally young and enthusiastic until he died in 1987, the words of the anthem have never changed. Only their emphasis. In the bus they were sung without much thought; a supplement to 'She'll be coming round the mountain' or to 'Nellie Deane'. Nowadays at the dinner when the dwindling company of survivors of McIndoe's Army rise to sing their anthem, Blackie's verse holds the quality of a hymn, and provides a solemn conclusion to a convivial dinner.

The mad Australians and the Canadians who built a separate wing are remembered with particular affection; Canadians and Australians who served in their own RCAF or RAAF squadrons or individually with RAF squadrons.

Volunteers from the Dominions of the British Empire, as their homelands were still proud to be known, had travelled across the world to defend the mother country.

Many of the survivors of their generation find it incomprehensible that the mother country should have so hastily begun the process of deserting her 'children' and Commonwealth trading preferences in favour of closer relations with France, a disappointing ally in war, and her former and brutal enemy, Germany. It should never be forgotten that the Canadians, the Aussies and the Kiwis had come to Britain in such numbers and with such zeal that soon they were in as much need of the Sty as the founding Maxillonians.

There were many more Canadian guinea pigs than Australians, New Zealanders or airmen from the other Empire countries. This was due to the immensity of the Empire (later Commonwealth) Air Training Scheme. As Canadian casualties increased, it grew plain that the bursting Sty, although already expanded, could not continue to offer them its especial facilities without swift extension of its original buildings and emergency huts.

Canada understood. She moved in her Royal Canadian Engineers. She provided her own materials. She built a large wing for the little hospital. She shipped her own doctors, surgeons and nursing sisters to East Grinstead and when Germany had been defeated, she shipped them all home to the Maritimes, the Prairies and the Rockies with equal speed and she presented her wing to the Queen Victoria (Cottage) Hospital of East Grinstead.

Work on the Canadian wing began in 1943 when Bomber Harris's ever increasing offensive against Germany took its toll of RCAF crews in dead and wounded. Even as the Canadian wing was being built Squadron Leader Ross Tilley, an RCAF surgeon, arrived at the Queen Victoria Hospital with an anaesthetist and three nursing sisters for attachment to McIndoe and his team for training. Once the wing was ready, Ross Tilley, known following promotion with great affection as the wingco – despite further promotion to group captain – received command.

On December 31, 1943, Clement Attlee, Labour deputy prime minister in Winston Churchill's coalition government attended the laying of the foundation stone.

An opening ceremony had been planned for July 12, 1944, when the first nine "fried, mashed and hash-browned" patients as the Canadians described their guinea pigs, were admitted. On the day V1 doodlebug flying-bombs appeared overhead and exploded in the vicinity.

Ross Tilley was in his early forties. He was from Brownsville, Ontario and the son of a doctor. He was reputed, aged twelve, to have assisted his father, also a doctor, by giving a patient an anaesthetic. As war came Ross was one of the very few plastic surgeons in Canada. Quiet and enigmatic, the wingco differed in most respects from the more extrovert Archie McIndoe. Each recognised the other's strengths and talents. The maestro particularly admired the artistry of the wingco's work on guinea pig hands and admired his talent for surgery which reduced the number of cases thought to require amputation.

Rita Donovan includes a perceptive study of the wingco in her book *As for the Canadians*: She describes him as "a quiet man of great authority, a calm, athletic, humorous man who could sit you down and talk to you or just listen as you went on. He was a constant in a world that had so rapidly changed. He was an excellent surgeon who told you he could repair your useless arm and you believed him. And when your hand, still bandaged, was doing a little better he was the man who accompanied you to the pub and watched with a smile as you successfully negotiated the pint to your lips."

A pint in a pub was only the beginning of Ross Tilley's acceptance of a duty of after care. As with McIndoe "he tapped into the curious energy that came from the Guinea Pig Club, realising that along with proper medical care it was the ticket to reintegration of these men into society." Whether or not a distinct dearth of psychiatrists in the guinea pig wards was due to the 'get on with life' ethos of the club the tale is told of a visiting shrink who, completing a tour of the guinea pig wards reported that his services were not needed.

Among the wingco's patients it remains a mystery that Jack Smith, a Canadian serving with No 36 Squadron, never received the George Medal for which he had been so strongly recommended by his group commander and commander-in-chief. Enormously popular John Campbell

Smith, pilot of O for Orange, a Wellington bomber, was briefed to take off from Chivenor in North Devon on Christmas Day, 1944. His mission was to search for a U-boat which had sunk a troopship off the Cherbourg peninsula. When hoarfrost was discovered on the Wellington's wings de-icing delayed take-off for more than an hour. The aircraft was not long airborne when the starboard engine caught fire and Jack ordered his crew to crash stations. He faced the dilemma that his Coastal Command Wellington was too low for the crew to bale out and too close to a populated area to jettison his depth charges.

Fire spread throughout the aircraft. It lost height rapidly and struck the ground killing the second pilot, navigator and wireless operator. Recovering consciousness Jack had difficulty getting clear of the wreckage. Though his clothes were on fire he climbed back into the cockpit aiming to rescue any of his crew he could find – until an explosion hurled him out of the fuselage and he lost consciousness again. In fact, his tail gunner and another crew member had also survived.

Jack suffered multiple burns and he and his fellow survivors were spotted by Avril Bower, an eleven-year-old schoolgirl who was returning in the family car from a Christmas visit to her grandparents. On New Year's Eve an air ambulance delivered him to a burns unit at RAF St Athan in Wales where he was told: "Well lad your flying days are over. We haven't got much to work with here, but we'll do the best we can." If the outlook was bleak there was at least the consolation that he could commiserate with Andre Browne the half Belgian pilot who had also been informed that little could be done for his hands.

However, there was a glimmer of hope when a nurse who had trained under McIndoe at the Queen Victoria Hospital urged Jack to seek another opinion. Refusing further treatment Jack insisted on being transferred to the Canadian wing, taking Andre Browne along for the ride. Following a four hour operation Jack came round to find Ross Tilley at his bedside. Before the wingco could say more than "How are you?", Jack asked anxiously "Have I still got my hands?" The wingco reassured him: "Of course you have." "Will I be able to fly again?" – "Of course you will. It's up to you." And Andre Browne? Appalled by earlier work on Andre's hands McIndoe, as has been narrated, admitted him. Years afterwards Jack was placed next to the wingco at a reunion dinner. "And did you fly again?" the surgeon asked gently. Jack slipped one of his repaired hands into a pocket and produced his private pilot's licence.

Distinguished from his Canadian namesake as 'Smithy', Ed Smith also flew again. Ed had led a charmed life as a bomber pilot until the night he was shot down in flames. Earlier than the enemy action which made him a guinea pig Ed was over Dunkirk in a No 102 Squadron Whitley bomber when the aircraft was hit by anti-aircraft fire. Although the fuel tanks had been damaged Ed pressed on and bombed Frankfurt. Unfortunately, the Whitley was an early version without self-sealing tanks and as Ed reached the Channel on his way home he was almost out of fuel. There was no option but to come down in the sea. Ed and his crew were picked up by Air Sea Rescue six hours later and subsequently admitted to membership of the Goldfish Club which had been formed by aircrew who had ended up in 'the drink'.

Following a week's leave Ed returned to operations and once again his target was Frankfurt. He was almost home to his base at Topcliffe in Yorkshire when, as the runway was illuminated for his landing an enemy night intruder got on his tail, blew off the Whitley's port rudder and set fire to its twin engines. While three of his crew died in the crash Ed, ablaze, was thrown out of the cockpit and an air-gunner who had survived beat out the flames.

When he regained consciousness a week later he celebrated his twenty-first birthday with two bottles of Guinness in hospital, an occasion which luckily coincided with one of McIndoe's periodic trawls of other hospitals for patients who would benefit from transfer to the Sty. McIndoe studied Ed's hands and knew that he stood a better chance of flying again in Ross Tilley's care. Ed was mended and returned to complete his interrupted bomber operational tour as a Halifax captain.

There can be few aircrew who qualified twice for membership of the Goldfish Club, an unsought honour which Ed achieved while 'resting' as an instructor in

Scotland. Ed's student pilot was at the controls when an engine failed and he took over and splashed down in a bay. Afterwards he completed a second tour on Halifaxes with No 424 Squadron and ended his war with a DSO and a Scottish wife. Returning to Canada Ed gained further distinction with the Department of Energy, Mines and Resources.

While some guinea pigs like Bertram Owen-Smith became doctors, Dr Lionel 'Hank' Hastings, another of the wingco's Canadian patients was destined to become a dentist. After working in the accounting department of Canada Packers near Toronto he joined the RCAF and qualified as a navigator. In May 1944 he joined No 98, an RAF Lancaster bomber squadron, at Dunsfold in Surrey and flew more than fifty operational sorties before being rested, ferrying Army personnel to and from the front during the Allied advance in north-west Europe.

On October 15 Hank became a guinea pig of the 'mashed' variety when one of his Avro Anson's two engines shut down outside Brussels in Belgium. He had lowered his undercarriage when the second engine failed and was attempting to glide the Anson into Courtrai airfield when it hit telephone wires and tipped into a bomb crater. While his navigator had strapped the Army passengers into crash positions before the impact Hank had not had time to secure himself and went head first into the controls and the windscreen.

Hank was shunted from hospital to hospital until, finally, he reached East Grinstead where Ross Tilley identified thirty-two facial fractures, three spinal fractures and broken arms and legs. After the wingco had completed the extensive work required by such multiple fractures, Hank resumed flying duties in Canada pending a posting to the Far East which was abandoned when the war against the Japanese ended. After qualifying as a dental surgeon Hank practised in Canada and served as a clinical instructor in China. Remaining active in the Guinea Pig Club he has twice served as chief guinea pig of the club's Canadian Wing.

Canadians were not inclined to identify themselves sentimentally with 'the old country' as readily as Australians or New Zealanders. In the early post-war years

Canadian guinea pigs kept a loose liaison with the Sty and with each other. But, the war in Europe over, they gave the maestro the ceremonial honour of hauling down their flag and dispersed.

In contrast with the Australians they were less emotional about guinea piggery. Their outlook was as practical as the purpose with which they had built their wing, made a film to prepare Canadian families for the return of their disfigured and crippled sons, and then left. However, as the years passed and they began to age, Canadian guinea pigs, having made their way in life, returned to East Grinstead in increasing numbers for the lost weekends and provided a warm welcome for all guinea pigs to reunions in Canada.

Yet, for all their haste to get home and put the war and its ravages behind them, some Canadians benefited from their association with influential and well connected members and friends of the mother organisation; a network which, for example enabled the realisation of Flight Lieutenant Gordon Fredericks's ambition to study engineering at Cambridge University.

Freddy, as he was known at the Sty, showed up for the second time when the Mosquito in which he was returning from an operational sortie crashed into the sea. After being delivered to an RAF hospital he wrote to McIndoe:

> "Dear Mac, Well, I've gone and done it again. It just came apart in me and sir. It's pretty hard to show a profit on me. I only hope it won't tie me up too long and cost me my chance to bag a hun.
>
> "The thing that has shaken me is landing in this concentration camp. I must say the place could do with a touch of your rationalising influence. It's quite a contrast to our beloved EG. The strangest part to my way of thinking is how little the boys seem to know about what is wrong with them and what is being done about it."

If ever there were evidence of the effectiveness of McIndoe's creed and the uniqueness of the Queen Victoria Hospital it lay in that statement.

In fact a remarkable change had been wrought in Freddy since his earlier encounter with McIndoe and the spirit of guinea piggery. He was no longer the embittered Freddy who had been admitted to the Sty for his first spell of seven months throughout which his sole aim was to obtain an early trip home. The second time round he could not wait to get back into the war.

Blackie, Russell and the maestro had been puzzled on Freddy's first appearance that he was not running true to form. Their usual experience was that, apart from wishing to get the job done, guinea pigs who were anywhere near fit to fly wished to return to their squadrons to dispel any idea that others might think they were hiding behind their wounds.

While the war situation remained critical and there was a shortage of trained aircrew, McIndoe saw it as his duty to get guinea pigs airborne again and was prepared to stretch a point under persistent requests to be released from hospital. So why during his first period at the Sty had Freddy contradicted the norm?

In time, Freddy admitted that having almost completed one tour of operations in an obsolescent torpedo-carrying Hampden, the type in which he had crashed into a petrol dump, he was extremely apprehensive about flying in a Hampden again. He told McIndoe that he felt it not unreasonable to seek a posting to a squadron equipped with an aircraft in which he could place confidence and to a Command in which the circumstances of his first mishap could not be duplicated.

McIndoe took the point immediately and asked Fredericks to be specific. "I would like to be posted to a Mosquito squadron" he said, "and I would prefer bomber Mosquitoes because I believe they give a little more scope to the observer."

A few days later McIndoe wrote personally on Freddie's behalf to Sammy Hoare, the Mosquito intruder ace: "My dear Hoare, I wonder if you would be good enough to see and talk with Flying Officer Gordon Fredericks, RCAF. He is a very experienced observer who had the misfortune to crash in a Hampden seven months ago, sustaining fairly severe burns, from which he has now completely recovered . . . his fancy seems to be in Mosquito work."

In the event Mossie or no Mossie a second mishap returned Freddie to the Sty for further repairs following which the Guinea Pig Club helped him up to Cambridge and through a number of financial vicissitudes until the boss was delighted to receive this note: "Dear Archie. Have a drink on me and see that John and Russell get one too. I got a First . . . My real thanks are to the club which made it possible."

McIndoe replied: "My dear Freddie. A thousand congratulations on your results. It is simply magnificent and everybody here is pleased beyond words. I am sorry that you are off to Canada so soon but I am sure you must be looking forward to it. In any case it has all been worthwhile *and the Club feel honoured by your success*."

Don Freeborn from Millbank, Ontario, was another Canadian guinea pig who built a successful post-war life. Some four weeks after opening his operational career as a Lancaster pilot in No 153 Squadron Don was raiding Stuttgart when the bomber was hit by flak, wounding him in the left thigh and almost blowing him out of his seat. Being almost over the target although he was bleeding, he ignored his injury and pressed home his attack.

Considering it unlikely the Halifax would make it home Don and the crew had opted to make for Switzerland where they aimed to bale out when Don discovered his parachute had been shredded by shrapnel. It had saved his life. When he offered to drop his crew over Switzerland before attempting the home trip they insisted: "If you're going to fly back for bacon and eggs we're sticking with you."

Don made an emergency landing at Manston on the Kent coast. Disconsolate about his condition and fearful he would lose a leg he was much comforted after reaching the Queen Victoria Hospital to be visited by "two amazing people, Bill Foxley and Les Wilkins". He recalled: "Their terribly burned faces and hands shocked me at first, then a quiet feeling of gratitude came over me and I thanked the Almighty that he had preserved me from such terrible burns. These two young men, just boys really, had the most outstanding morale I had ever seen in my life and retained that spirit throughout their ordeals at East Grinstead."

Don was awarded an immediate DFC for bombing the target and saving his crew. After being repaired sufficiently with skin grafts he resumed operational flying. After four more trips his Lancaster was shot down by a night fighter over Holland in January 1945. As the remainder of the crew baled out – the navigator's parachute failing to open – Don and his rear-gunner stayed put until the gunner had taken revenge on the night fighter, earning as a result a Bar to his DFC. After spending another seventeen years in the RCAF Don joined Canadair as a test pilot.

Nobody said: "Make Jack Allaway the star of a film, it is the only occupational therapy which will return him to people." Not even Blackie. Where they believed it would help, the boss and Blackie indulged guinea pig fancies. However, resourceful as they were and notwithstanding McIndoe's carefully nourished connections in the world of entertainment, they would have been exercised to arrange a starring role for Jack Allaway, who had lost much of his face in a bomber crash. Fortuitously, the Canadian government, concerned about public reaction to the arrival of the first repatriated Canadian guinea pig, provided Jack with this unlikely opportunity.

Canada commissioned *New Faces for Old*, a film documentary aimed at preparing Canadians at home for the return of its disfigured and mutilated servicemen but when the film unit arrived at the Sty no Canadian pig was sufficiently advanced in repair to take the lead role. Jack Allaway, whose self-consciousness had been worrying Blackie and the boss, got the part. Sewing Canadian shoulder flashes and badges on to Jack's service tunic, a nurse converted the sergeant from Birmingham into an 'acting' Canadian. Thus, the documentary served the double purpose of restoring Jack's confidence and reassuring Canadians from Moncton to Medicine Hat that their boys were being well cared for in a very English sounding place named East Grinstead. Jack's stardom marked the beginning of more than half a century of service to the Guinea Pig Club of which in its sixtieth anniversary year he remains chief executive responsible for welfare.

Enthusiasm in any man is an enormous personal asset. In a guinea pig it is gold. To encounter prancing enthusiasm in a disfigured and maimed man, is the uplift equivalent of a pint of Black Velvet on the morning after the night of the reunion dinner. Some guinea pigs were born dour and despite all the efforts of Blackie, Archie and Russell and the spirit of guinea piggery at East Grinstead they remained so.

Theirs was the advantage when the outlook was bleak. They accepted the downs the more easily. But meet a guinea pig who is an enthusiast and one is swept along with the tide race.

Alan Morgan, whose down temporarily destroyed him, became one of the club's great enthusiasts. His enthusiasm for his jig-boring machine, his bouncing description of its infinite potentialities, his thanksgiving that with no fingers, half a thumb on one hand and a whole thumb on the other, he could work to 0.00015 inch on a jig-boring machine, had to be experienced to be believed. Jack Allaway, describing the profitable sale of his first shop in Birmingham and how business prospects opened out for him at Crawley, nearby the Sty in Sussex, is another great guinea pig enthusiast. But he had experienced his down and not always had it been thus.

One learns this when Jack's eyes grow serious within the rings of pale, motionless skin with which McIndoe repaired his face and as he feels contemplatively down his new nose, which was raised by pedicle from the skin of his chest and says quietly: "One of the best Mac did, isn't it? But he was lucky with my grafts. Everything took. It was always 'send for Jack Allaway' when Archie wanted to show his handiwork off." No wonder he was a natural for the Canadian film.

Jack was a bomber wireless operator/air-gunner. He had returned on October 10, 1942, from a shipping strike in the Skagerrak when a Ju 88 intruder sneaked-up on the Hampden's tail and shot it down as it was about to land in Norfolk:

"We were making our approach when I saw the tracers. We caught fire and I thought 'this is the end'. When I realised I had survived the crash, I found I couldn't open the cupola above me. My hands were burned. I was not frightened. I thought of mother at home. I just thought 'I wonder what she's going to think when I've gone'. Honestly, I was quite prepared to stay there and wait. I heard a scream. I suppose it was the navigator. Then I looked down and saw daylight. I dropped through the hole into a ditch and scrambled into a ploughed field. My hands had been badly burned because I'd taken my gloves off and was getting my gear together, thinking 'well that's another one safely over' – my twenty-fifth in fact."

Jack spent six months at the RAF hospital, Ely, before removal to the Sty:

> "Wing Commander George Morley did my temporary eyelids there and Archie McIndoe trimmed them up later. Towards the end of my time at Ely I grew pretty impatient. I wanted them to hurry up but with contraction from burns you can't hurry. You've got to wait, for instance, for your eyelids to finish their contraction. So there you are with whopping great eyelids and wondering whether you'll always look like that."

"I was so anxious", Jack said, "that one day Archie brought along a chap who'd been through it before the war. 'This is what you'll be like', he said, 'but it will take time.' See my nose. That's a very good nose, I reckon, but it took twelve months. There it was like a lump of plasticine to begin with. Archie had to sculpture it, take the fat away, put in the nostrils."

In common with his fellow guinea pigs and most people, Jack Allaway had never considered what burning does to a body. It was something aircrew did not begin to think about. The degree of some of the guinea pigs' burns is evidence of the distressing result of a failure to rationalise between acceptance of the danger of fire and the encumbrance of protective gloves, helmets and goggles.

Tom Gleave's goggles were up but he was wearing his favourite gloves "a thin, pansy unofficial type", he said. Even with this protection his fingertips were so burned that, by removing his fingerprints, the enemy provided him with a passport to undetectable burglary had he wished to resort to crime. Nevertheless, his hands were only slightly crippled. Jack Mann's goggles were up when, eyes tight shut, he crash-landed his blazing Spitfire . . . Jack Allaway had taken his gloves off and was putting his gear away . . . The evidence repeats and repeats itself.

If, however, aircrew refusal to accept the possibility of severe burning and their lack of appreciation of the effects of burning led in many cases to serious wounds – the

degree of which might sometimes have been lessened –
correspondingly, it reduced awareness as they lay
bandaged in hospital of the true extent of the ravages of the
fire which had consumed them.

"You don't realise for quite a while that you are going to
look different", Jack Allaway said. "If you have ever seen a
burned man before, you wonder, 'what's happened to him'
and you tend to think that perhaps he was born like it."
This, Jack believes, helps to explain why so many people
are so surprised, initially, when they meet guinea pigs who
are happily married and have children who are among the
most handsome in the land. Jack remembered:

> "It's when you get a bit better, that you begin to think,
> 'well, perhaps I do look a bit different.' It was at Ely
> where, unlike East Grinstead, there was not a ward full
> of other guinea pigs to help you get used to the idea,
> that I caught the reflection of myself in sister's office
> window from twenty feet away. I was too scared to go
> any closer and I turned away quickly. I thought, 'you
> look like a chimpanzee'. That was because I was
> looking straight at my nostrils.
>
> "At first when I was well enough to go to the toilet
> I couldn't bring myself to look in the mirror. Then I
> took a quick peep, a very quick peep. I thought, 'It's
> just not you. It's like looking at somebody else.' I was
> too scared to take a second look. Next time I was a bit
> more daring. I took a closer look and looked just a little
> longer. It was very odd. I felt the same person and yet
> it just wasn't me. Can you imagine? You know what
> you look like. You go to a mirror and you see someone
> quite different. And, just as strange, your fingers are
> locked in one position and yet they feel the same as
> they were before being burned.
>
> "Slowly you come to accept it. Then you begin to
> say, 'well, I'm not too bad.' Then you find the courage
> to really study yourself at different angles and when
> you get to East Grinstead where there are so many
> others, you find yourself saying 'and I'm certainly not
> as bad as poor old so and so.' And very soon, when you
> begin to get out and about you make your greatest
> discovery. You find that girls don't go for good looks.

The good looking fellow can't just click his fingers and
they all come running. They don't."

With some guinea pigs it was very different. Letters were
received at the Sty from women who preferred disfigured
men not for their great hearts but from a perverse attraction
for their scars and weals. When after meeting a particular
guinea pig his admirer became more attentive the patient
in question was asked discreetly to what extent he was
interested in her. If he indicated he desired no further
contact she was brushed firmly off.

Later, after the film which the Canadians made had
helped to restore Jack's confidence, Billy Butlin stepped in
with an offer which was to contribute to the increase of
confidence among a number of guinea pigs. He offered
them jobs at his holiday camps. At the Clacton camp Jack
met Joan who, following demobilisation from the ATS, was
working there as a waitress. They married and had piglets.

* * *

That certain national characteristics of Australians, not
least their rugged nature, aggressive self-reliance, and
readiness to question authority and idiotic red tape,
equipped them admirably when they became guinea pigs
was soon evident. Blackie, whose success in taming an
Australian flying-boat squadron at Plymouth had marked
him as the man for the Sty, and Archie McIndoe, from New
Zealand, reckoned that every Australian who was
unfortunate enough to qualify for membership of the club
would be an asset.

They were not to be disappointed. Australian guinea
pigs relished the rankless society at the Sty and in the
Guinea Pig Club since the war. The passage of time and
distance – not so much a factor as air travel improved – has
not dimmed their continuing interest in the club and
concern for their fellow members and their fortitude has
remained an inspiration to the club.

Adrian 'King' Cole, an Australian air vice-marshal, was
a particular favourite of British guinea pigs. Known as
King throughout the hospital he was wounded as an air
forward commander in the disastrous Dieppe raid of 1942.

King's jaw was fractured and he collected a piece of German shell in his back when a shore battery shell landed on the bridge of the control ship, *Calpe*. From Haslar naval hospital King Cole was rushed to East Grinstead, where, "Archie had me patched up within minutes and next day, after a little forcing, agreed to have me fit in eighteen days ready to take on a group in Northern Ireland." Cole had stressed the need for haste to McIndoe because, in taking up the appointment, he would become the first Australian to command such a large RAF unit. King Cole recalled: "He did this but it was so close to time that on the morning of the eighteenth day he drove me to his Harley Street rooms, took off the bandages and dried up a large scar with methylated spirits."

When King arrived at the Sty he had asked McIndoe: "How long will it take?" The surgeon replied: "With bone rot and the usual troubles of fractured jaws, perhaps three to four months." Cole countered: "Rot, make it three weeks." On the eighteenth day, McIndoe rushed the air vice-marshal from Harley Street to the medical board – which generally took two days. King Cole noted: "We got there at 10 a.m. and by 11.30 a.m. were having tea in the doctors' rest room and I took off 'fit' from Northolt for Northern Ireland at 2.30 p.m. . . . Archie and I became close friends and corresponded regularly till his death . . . I formed the opinion that Archie McIndoe was nearer to God than anyone I'd ever met in two wars and the good he did at that hospital was easily assessed by the love of his patients and the idolisation ever since."

Lest King's easy going readiness to be one of the crowd at the Sty leaves an impression that the Guinea Pig Club's equality of rank was almost entirely due to a more relaxed relationship between officers and men in Empire forces or because McIndoe was a New Zealander, credit is also due to a very basic bit of British enamelware, the bath.

In the beginning there had been but one ward and one saline bath in which the 'bathroom boys', as guinea pigs called the attendants, treated burned officers, men and civilians. The salt bath sounds magnificent, all marbled and tiled like a bath at a spa. In fact it was a very ordinary English bath, as chipped and naked as baths exposed after air-raids, perched hazardously among the ruins of bombed-out homes.

The salt bath stood in a corner of Ward 3. In it, shielded by ship's canvas screens on runners, a guinea pig found his relief be he air vice-marshal or AC2. Tom Gleave said: "They were all fried bodies to Sergeant Salmon and his orderlies who gently lowered them into the salt bath and as gently lifted them out." Here, then, was the true birthplace of the rankless, classless society and, incidentally, where at least one guinea pig romance blossomed. Betty Andrews, who also bathed guinea pigs as tenderly as babies at bedtime married 'Hoke' Mahn, a legless American airman who, sadly, was to die peacefully shortly after his surgery repair had been completed.

All ranks, and all races benefited from the salt bath and guinea piggery, British and Empire guinea pigs, the Americans, one Russian and other foreign aircrew who, unlucky to have been burned, were fortunate in fetching up at the Queen Victoria Hospital.

Vladimir Rasumov or 'Raz', the sole Red Air Force guinea pig, had been found in Germany by the Army and subsequently delivered to East Grinstead because he had been burned and the Germans had started his plastic surgery. Raz had been attacking a German bomber when a fighter bounced him and he baled out of his blazing Yak. The question of what Raz should wear presented a unique problem. He arrived in a hand-me-down khaki battle dress and the maestro was unwilling to approach the Russian Embassy for an appropriate Russian uniform, for fear that his patient would be removed before his surgery had been completed.

It appeared that Raz was the equivalent of a flight lieutenant and his fellow guinea pigs decided that he should wear the uniform and brevet of an RAF flight lieutenant. Dressed for all the world as an RAF officer the Russian fighter pilot accompanied his fellows to pubs, cinemas and people's homes and to many parties. Eventually, Raz was repatriated and although the Guinea Pig Club attempted to reach him at his father's address in Russia there was no further contact.

* * *

"Here's your problem. Deal with it." Bluntly, McIndoe addressed a party of aircraft industrialists who were visiting the hospital and meeting guinea pigs for the first time. *Their* problem, as they understood it, was supplying the air force through the Ministry of Aircraft Production with new aircraft for the operational squadrons where men who had become guinea pigs were replaced by fresh, unscathed aircrew from the Empire air training schools. Thus, customarily brisk and uncompromising, McIndoe confronted his high powered visitors with patients in various stages of repair and threw *his* problem at the visitors.

The plane makers did not disappoint him. They equipped a mini works within the hospital, the most unusual of the many cottage industry workshops set up in wartime Britain. It was a workshop where men who were trying to get what remained of their hands, to feel, to move, and to grasp again, manufactured components for the bombers and fighters which their successors and, indeed, some of them would fly against the Germans and the Japanese.

The workshop was an advanced conception of occupational therapy resulting from lessons learned from answers to earlier mistakes. It became a great success because, like the founding and development of the club, it was an idea which enthused the guinea pigs following their disenchantment with earlier attempts to introduce occupational therapy.

Assembly of a pathetic little circle of fighter pilots knitting and rug making or the despatch to factories of guinea pigs resting between surgical operations had not been successful. The former practice had proved frustrating, if not humiliating, to men who were not only dismayed that they were out of the battle, but had also begun to see themselves as institutionalised wrecks, condemned to scarves, hearth mats and tea cosies for the rest of their lives. "But for pleasing the Old Man, I wouldn't have done it," Geoff Page commented to Blackie.

The subsequent work-alongside-the-workers scheme, had appeared ideal in theory, but proved impracticable. Management took one look at the mutilated men, felt sorry and guilty and decided that neither money nor effort be spared to show them a good time. A guinea pig had to be particularly strong-minded to resist the primrose path which the scheme opened up. Some gladly returned to their hospital beds for more reasons than that the slab beckoned for a further stage in their repair.

Blackie was caustic about the scheme, yet it would not be balanced to pass forward to his assessment of its value to some guinea pigs, without offering at least two examples of the extent to which those who applied themselves conscientiously, benefited. Gordon Fredericks, the Canadian observer who had been burned in a Hampden crash, mended and following a Mosquito mishap, returned to the Sty, and was employed by Reid and Sigrist's electrical and aeronautical engineering factory at New Malden, wrote to McIndoe in July 1943:

> "You have seen the improvement in my hands so there is no need for me to stress the real benefit that this job has been to me on the medical side. Something that may not have been so apparent is the morale building effect of working among people who are really putting their backs into the war effort and turning out a first class product."

Pilot Officer George Phillipi, the first war Colonel who had brought Smith-Barry to the Sty, received the following note at the Air Ministry from Flying Officer Mills in early 1942: "If possible I shall be grateful if you could obtain some factory or other work for me before I return to the squadron as I shall be quite useless there really."

Blackie's adverse opinion of the scheme, as declared in *Guinea Pig*, ran:

> "The Guinea Pig was packed off to a factory, generally near his home. There, unfortunately, unless he was a particularly strong-minded type and well and truly married, habits were formed which were bad. Gradually the pig's lower nature triumphed and the situation arose of him requiring sick leave before his return from rehabilitation. Equally, MAP [reference to the scheme undertaken in Ministry of Aircraft Production factories] was not satisfactory from the

factory manager's point of view. He was worried by the thought of what to do with the guinea pig and generally hit on the not very bright idea of treating him to life with a capital 'L'. The result . . . MAP was not an unqualified success."

While the high life provided by factory management was effective in helping guinea pigs to overcome inhibitions, it was no way to prepare them to return to service life or for resettlement. "They lost", Blackie wrote, "their sense of responsibility and their desire for the ordinary routine of life." Bringing the workshop to the hospital helped to answer these very human problems. It was an adventurous and groundbreaking exercise and conformed to the spirit of guinea piggery which had been nurtured at the Sty since the club's foundation.

In these circumstances the scheme quickly became a success and led to an extension at Marchwood Park, a Hampshire mansion, where however, celebrating their liberation from the least disciplined hospital in Britain, some guinea pigs were content to relax and be more playful than industrious. Jack Allaway held the view that Marchwood Park prepared him well for his holiday camp experience at Butlins though upon reflection he agreed with most guinea pigs that in some respects he was being a trifle unfair to Billy Butlin who would not have permitted panties on his flagstaff and round-the-clock high jinks.

Marchwood Park was more than a holiday camp. It was, George Taylor remembered, "like Christmas all the time." The guinea pigs turned Marchwood into one long party, transferring to it the Sty's tradition of days and nights of partying. There was the occasion when Paddy Naismith, one of the Marchwood contingent's greatest supporters arranged a week-long party at London's Dorchester Hotel.

Indeed, Marchwood Park holds an honoured place in guinea pig memory as a monument to the wilder moments of guinea piggery and those responsible for them, an ironic result of McIndoe's original intention to use Marchwood for restful convalescence from the Sty where guinea pigs could be gradually re-introduced to service discipline.

* * *

In wartime plastic surgery cases which necessitated a long series of operations, it was essential to stay the knife between operations while grafts settled down. The aircraft factory scheme had not, as has been explained, been satisfactory and the cottage industry workshop had been restricted to guinea pigs at the hospital. These drawbacks, as McIndoe described them "agitated and distracted" him in his quest to occupy and place guinea pigs during the long term treatment of severe burns.

They could, perhaps, have been dispersed among existing Service convalescent homes, but the boss did not wish to lose touch or some measure of control nor to burden unwary staff with the exceptional problems attached to guinea pigs. He wanted his guinea pigs in one place where he could maintain contact and keep a fatherly eye.

Marchwood Park was the answer and it was many years before McIndoe let slip how in a manner wholly in keeping with the spirit of the Guinea Pig Club, it came about. He said: "George Phillipi and I nearly ruined ourselves entertaining half the RAF High Command to dinner at Claridges in order to ram Marchwood Park down their necks and especially to keep it under the control of P.5." [Air Ministry section looking after guinea pig affairs.]

So that Marchwood marched in step with how things were done at the Sty Blackie installed Johnnie Higdon, a sergeant so much in Blackie's style that he very soon became Marchwood's own Blackie. It may seem oddly irregular that the physical training instructor who had thought originally that he was expected to do 'knees bend' with legless men could take his pick from the non-commissioned officers of the RAF but this was typical of the Guinea Pig Club's non-conformist approach. Blackie had first encountered Johnnie as the sergeant who had helped him tame the boisterous Australians at Plymouth.

McIndoe, Blackie and Russell were masters of the art of short-circuiting official machinery and red tape to arrive speedily at a correct solution. Their old boy network was as strong as a warship's hemp hawser. McIndoe was a powerful networker who skillfully used his friends at court though the knowledge that he had call on them was sufficient to get what he wanted. The combination of the personal power of the maestro and the clout of the club became an irresistible force and frequently resulted in the despair of tidy-minded officials faced with squaring off the paper work after the whirlwind.

Occasionally, a guinea pig was fortunate enough to experience an exceptional occupational respite break between runs of surgery. Bill Simpson contacted the Army intelligence major who had debriefed him when he returned from France and obtained an introduction to Colonel Maurice Buckmaster, head of the Special Operations Executive (SOE) section responsible for clandestine activities in France.

Although Bill's somewhat ambitious request to return to France and assist in the selection of landing grounds for delivering agents and dropping zones for Resistance weapons and supplies was refused, his initiative was rewarded with an operations post at SOE's Norgeby House, Baker Street, London office.

One of his tasks was to liaise with RAF squadrons designated to SOE. He was still clumsy with the methods he had adopted to use a telephone but since as little as possible at Norgeby House was committed to paper he managed to get by, holding a flat pencil between the remains of the first and second fingers of his right hand.

Despite tiresome physical limitations Bill was cheered by being useful in such an unusual capacity and savoured the irony of resuming hostilities against an enemy who had so grudgingly allowed him to return home on the grounds that he was of no further military use. There was the further boost that he received the promotion to squadron leader which his courage and bravery, evidenced by a DFC ribbon, had delayed.

Even so the limitations of his injuries continued to frustrate him, compelling him for instance to hold bus change between finger stumps. He was also embarrassed by the difficulties of giving and returning the numerous and obligatory salutes required of street encounters with those senior and junior to himself. When possible he re-routed himself to avoid the saluting nightmares presented by the prevalence of senior officers in Whitehall and the ritual recognition of his rank by sentries.

Yet, such traumas were trivial compared with the daily

hazards of steps to the tops of buses, office and home stairs, door handles and coping with buttons, zips and fasteners in lavatories and with the London blackout which presented "a pit of fear". He also feared falling and being unable to get up again.

In time, Bill began to adapt to his condition and learned to live with it as best he could. Serving with SOE he was keen to visit an airfield where agents were assembled for despatch in Westland Lysander, Lockheed Hudson and Handley Page Halifax aircraft. Persistence eventually overcame his superiors' initial fears that his appearance might unsettle 'Joes', as agents were known to aircrew who landed or dropped them in enemy-occupied territory.

Authorisation of regular airfield visits to witness the despatch of Joes encouraged Bill to push his luck further. Feeling he had nothing to lose he offered to be landed in France and attempt to pass himself off as a wounded French soldier. On parole in France before being repatriated Yvonne, a spirited girl with underground connections, had cared for him in her apartment above a brothel and promised to shelter him if he returned. But SOE, while prepared to entrust him with considerable responsibility in Baker Street, drew the line at this.

When, after six months, Bill was recalled to the Queen Victoria Hospital it was a wrench to leave the nerve centre of the organisation Winston Churchill, the wartime prime minister, had directed to "set Europe ablaze". But he consoled himself that a new thumb would be of greater use in the future than remaining – in SOE terms – a 'Baker Street Irregular'.

Bill re-accustomed himself to the familiar Ward 3 routine, allowing plenty of time to alternate a daydream that he had a home and children with a conviction that he would never fall in love again – until a new nurse appeared at his bedside. Monica swept into the ward, "proud and shining and brimming over with the confidence of attraction and charm." Bill noted: "She wore her small white cap set high atop her waving hair, jauntily as was the fashion . . . warmth and sunlight enfolded her. They were in the sparkle of her eyes, in the curves of her figure, in her smile and in her laughter, in her voice that was sweet and caressing."

He had decided it would be better to put this seemingly unattainable angel out of his mind when, as it happened, a serious bout of bronchitis removed her for some weeks. But Monica returned and Bill was moved by her nursing skills and care of her patients. He decided she was neither as proud nor aloof as he had thought. Although he hardly knew her he realised he was falling deeply in love and as the couple roamed the Sussex countryside she accepted him. In the first blissful rapture Bill and Monica were blind to the differences which separated them "like mountain gorges" but the marriage was not to fail until long after it had produced a son and a daughter.

Meanwhile, Bill's resolution to accept the pain and boredom of further and extensive surgery was rewarded sooner than he had dared hope. Offered the choice of an administrative post or being invalided from the Service, he selected the latter taking with him a 100 per cent disability pension and accepting a job from Lord Beaverbrook as a reporter on the *Sunday Express*. Ingeniously, he sought to overcome the mechanical problems of taking notes, inserting carbons and typing copy. Very soon he was an accredited war correspondent.

Bill preferred not to wear, as he was entitled, an officer's uniform with green and gold war correspondent insignia when he visited fighter squadrons during the June 1944, invasion of Normandy and was reunited with Geoff Page who, despite his crippled hands, had resumed operational flying for a second time.

A year earlier Page, employing every ounce of his considerable charm, had persuaded the Service that he could control a fighter with his damaged fingers and had been posted to North Africa where the desert sun soon demonstrated that its heat was incompatible with his skin grafts. Posted home Page was teamed at the Air Fighting Development Unit (AFDU), Wittering, Hunts, with Squadron Leader James MacLachlan, a one armed ace with a DSO and DFC and two Bars, to evaluate Allied fighter aircraft.

On June 29, 1943, the pair piloting P51 Mustang long-range fighters – MacLachlan flying with an artificial arm clamped to his aircraft's throttle lever – shot down a total of six enemy aircraft between them. But this action and

Bill's interlude with SOE were behind them when Bill,
notebook at the ready, called on Geoff at his Ford, Sussex,
fighter station.

Geoff eyed the results of McIndoe's rhinoplasty. "The old
coconut is settling down nicely." Three years earlier at the
historic grogging party Geoff had minuted the Guinea Pig
Club's founding meeting. Now, employing the banter of
the Sty, he sought to help Bill over his disappointment that
he was reporting a fellow guinea pig's current operational
exploits rather than sharing them. For his part Geoff found
comfort in confiding in a fellow guinea pig who would
understand his dismay at the awkwardness of his crooked
and stiff fingers and the painful and bleeding results of
knocking against things in a fighter cockpit.

Sublimating his deep desire to follow Geoff and fly
operationally again, Bill put his mind to producing the
good newspaper story that Geoff provided. Here was a
twenty-four-year-old guinea pig commanding a fighter
wing and who, despite forty surgical operations, was much
feared by the enemy. Bill did him justice, though in the
summer of 1944 Geoff had yet to accumulate his final score
of at least seventeen enemy aircraft destroyed and be
awarded the DSO he was to add to his DFC and Bar.

Bill's *Sunday Express* article could not have been more
timely. Shortly after it appeared Geoff was attacking
ground targets near the Arnhem bridgehead in Holland
when he was wounded by anti-aircraft fire, crash-landed
and returned to hospital. The incident closed his fighting
war and in the New Year of 1945 the Air Ministry sent him
on a public relations speaking tour of the United States. He
was being lionised in Hollywood when he met and fell in
love with Pauline, the attractive and vivacious daughter of
Nigel Bruce, and in the next year married her. They were to
have two sons and a daughter. As for Bill Simpson, his
career as an author and journalist blossomed and he went
on to spend much of the rest of his civilian life in public
relations, notably at British European Airways.

CHAPTER NINE

"We do well to remember that the privilege of dying for one's country is not equal to the privilege of living for it."

"Simple research has shown", Blackie wrote to a friend, "that severe burning has no effect on reproduction and the guinea pigs are satisfactorily holding their own biologically, if not actually increasing their numbers . . . there are many married guinea pigs and they have just over two children each."

Eileen and Dickie Richardson have *exactly* two children. Twins. If any of those insensitive and thoughtless people who questioned Jean and Reg Hyde's decision to breed guinea piglets had met Heather and Keith Richardson, bonnie babies some fifty years ago, they would have been ashamed of their idiotic fear that guinea pig children might inherit the disfigurement of their fathers.

The flames which consumed Dickie's Lancaster after it had bombed a German panzer depot during the Allied advance through north-west Europe, not only burned away most of his face but also blinded him in both eyes. This, of course, did not prevent him from contributing to the birth, eyesight and handsome features of Heather and Keith – although, as Dickie said: "You'd be surprised at the number of people who think that just because you are disfigured and blind you must be a congenital idiot."

Nothing infuriated Dickie more than the quiet whispering of people who, because he is blind thought he was unable to see them:

"You go into a pub and you hear them saying, 'Does he drink? Would he rather sit down?' Such people are very annoying. But I feel sorry for the other sort, the people who feel too embarrassed to talk to you. Go on a long train journey and they never say a word. I was three and a half hours on a train. One man said, 'Do you mind if I open the window?' and when he had left the carriage another man said 'Do you mind if I shut the window?' A blind man welcomes a conversation.

"Mind you now that the new plastic eyes have come in and can be fixed in the socket so that you can move them about just like real eyes it's getting easier. The new eyes are so good that sometimes people don't realise you are blind. I was on a train when another passenger offered me a paper to read. When that happens one cannot embarrass people by telling them you're blind. One simply says, 'No thank you very much. I've seen it.'"

Sometimes, Dickie wondered how his life would have developed had the German anti-aircraft gunners missed his Lancaster. As the sole survivor of the crew he had a very strong sense of his good fortune in surviving. He never discovered how he escaped, or how with his clothes on fire he floated on his parachute onto a French farm.

Dickie was the bomber's wireless operator. He remembered hearing the skipper giving the order to abandon. He was not wearing his parachute, but managed to put it on as the bomber blazed before stumbling towards the rear door to make his escape. But he fell flat into the flames and that is all he knew until he found himself on the ground and still burning. His right hand, which had been almost burned away, was in a clenched position and clutching the rip-cord. Dickie had no idea how he left the Lancaster.

He thought, however, that as he fell into the flames he might have been clutching at the rip-cord, that possibly there was an explosion in which he was thrown clear and in which his hand jerked his parachute open. Alternatively, another member of the crew might have picked him up and thrown him out and then failed to escape himself. Whatever the explanation it was some time before the crew's relatives knew whose son had survived. Identification of such a grievously burned airman as Dickie was all the more puzzling because Dickie had taken a shower before take-off and forgotten to replace his identity disc.

Dickie was to encounter a special problem not common to the majority of sightless men. Having lost his right hand and much of the left he was without the fingers to learn braille. However, the Guinea Pig Club helped to establish him in a sweets and tobacco shop in Worcester where his pre-war employment had been as a telegraph boy and postman, and enabled him to find his way around his home town. Unable to make use of braille or equipment which can assist sightless people to make notes and play them back, he began to develop a retentive memory. When a customer asked for humbugs he could go straight to the humbug jar and he knew exactly where to find any particular brand of cigarettes.

Unfortunately, some customers took advantage of Dickie and his takings began to show figures that did not always match his sales. So St Dunstan's trained him to operate a telephone switchboard which he managed to do by making quick darting movements with his one incomplete hand.

Dickie worked as the switchboard operator at St Dunstan's near Brighton, but do not assume that St Dunstan's gave him the job out of kindness. Dickie Richardson was the best man for the job and was paid the going rate, being reckoned to be more efficient than a sighted and unmaimed operator. The memory which blindness had improved enabled him to retain telephone numbers, his sole aid being a tape-recorder which enabled him to pass on verbatim messages.

Generally, McIndoe insisted upon professional investigation of the soundness of a guinea pig's preferred occupation before supporting Blackie and Russell's recommendations to spend club money or make a case to the RAF Benevolent Fund for help in realising a guinea pig's dream. In this respect the club in its early days was fortunate in Alfred Wagg's acceptance of the honorary treasurership. Resident in East Grinstead this shrewd merchant and investment banker was readily available to offer worldly wisdom, financial advice and to introduce Cyril 'Harve' Harvey of his company Helbert Wagg, later Schroeder Wagg, as his successor.

Alfred Wagg refused to condone schemes which seemed madcap when considered outside the euphoric world of

guinea piggery and the Sty. But when occasionally the club
pigeon-holed his counsel in conformity with its overriding
principle that a guinea pig be given the chance to prove to
himself what he could or could not do, he accepted the
decision. He was not, however, averse to issuing a
humorous warning for the record – and was often right.

At one stage the club consulted Alfred upon the
advisability of placing guinea pigs as publicans. At the end
of a long and careful consideration of this question he
concluded: "I have checked with Mr Lambert, formerly my
butler, whose opinion owing to his considerable
shrewdness, I have always been in the habit of asking. His
comment was: 'If I had all the money in the world I would
not start anybody up in a pub today.'"

In the event the club chose to ignore the advice of
Alfred's butler and assisted several members to exchange
their customary places at the bar for the other side where
the optics were a great temptation. But in at least one case
Alfred's butler seemed at first to have had the last laugh
until 'Chiefy' Adams, after much trial and tribulation,
settled down as an excellent landlord at The Royal Oak,
Croydon, a pub which suited Chiefy's personality.

* * *

Nobody at the annual dinner could remember very much
about Roy Lane. Joe Biel, the Pole sitting opposite, said he
had never heard of him. Blind Dickie Richardson, waiting
for Joe to finish cutting up a portion of turkey, could not
recall a guinea pig of that name. But John Banham, large
and executive-looking, a Battle of Britain fighter pilot who
became a brewer, thought back to 1940 and 1941. "Very
early. Yes, we called him Lulu. Apart from that I cannot tell
you much. Nice chap. Does Tom know?" Tom Gleave
didn't know.

Squadron Leader Lane was a forgotten guinea pig, one of
the club's lesser known warriors, but he merits more than
passing acknowledgement, particularly because he was
one of the intrepid guinea pigs who returned to operational
flying and subsequently lost their lives. 'Lulu' Lane's
exploits, though largely unremembered by his fellow
guinea pigs, rank high in the premier league of so many

brave and courageous men.

His story begins on July 13, 1940, two days after the official date for the beginning of the Battle of Britain, as a short service commission fighter pilot in No 43 Squadron, the famous 'Fighting Cocks'. After destroying a Ju 87 Stuka dive bomber on August 18 he was attacking He 111 bombers over Portsmouth on August 26th when his Hurricane was shot down and crashed. Let Roy tell the story of what happened that day and how he qualified for membership of the Guinea Pig Club:

"We climbed to the height ordered on the course and presently we sighted two formations of 30 Heinkels, each protected by roughly 50 Me 109s. We carried out the normal head-on attack, but in this instance the bombers didn't break their formation and it was our squadron that had to break instead, thereby scattering our aircraft all over the sky.

"I continued my attack too long and had to break off underneath the bombers, coming out the other end among their fighters. I managed to get straight through this lot without any of them attacking me and I climbed straight up again to get in a better position to attack the bombers. As I did so I noticed that one bomber formation was leaving and heading back towards the coast of France. These bombers were still a considerable height above me which meant that I had to climb as fast as I could . . .

"Behind the bombers were about five or six Me 110 fighters and as I was directly below them I thought they would probably not see me as I attacked the bombers. I took a good chance on this, keeping a sharp look-out in my mirror. Unfortunately as I was about to open fire on a bomber – and due to the fact that I was unable to take any evasive action – one of the Nazi fighters got me in his sights and my plane was hit in the engine. I heard two loud explosions and I guessed I'd been hit pretty badly. As I pushed the cockpit cover back I passed out through lack of oxygen. My oxygen apparatus had been badly damaged when my plane was hit.

"As I fainted I saw a dim red glow in front of my eyes – but I didn't understand what this was until I came to at a lower altitude. I found that my Hurricane was not only on fire but was diving upside down. Luckily I was hanging by my straps which enabled me to keep my face out of the flames a good deal. Even so I was unable to open my eyes due to the intense heat and I tried to operate the quick release pin so that I could fall out of the aircraft and use my parachute. For some reason this didn't work so I tried rolling my plane right way up. But this was unsuccessful due to the rolling motion of the aircraft blowing the flames still hotter. Eventually I got so tired of struggling to get out and I was so frightened, that I just gave up the ghost and I really began to think I was in hell.

"Shortly after this – I don't know how long after – I realised that things were much cooler. So I opened my eyes – to find there was no aeroplane around me. I think that the straps must have burned through, allowing me to fall out. I didn't wait long to admire the scenery, but began to see about opening my parachute. On looking around I discovered that it wasn't on me. As I knew I had it when I started I began to think it had been burned off me, but through force of habit I put my right arm on my left hip where the ripcord should be and I found something there. I gave it the hell of a tug, and then there was a violent crack and the canopy opened. I quickly discovered that I was upside down in the parachute, suspended by the ankles. Either the shoulder straps had burned through or they came off when I was struggling to get out of the plane. At all events I was falling upside down with the harness of the chute entangled in my flying boots. I was very glad indeed that I had on a pair of boots that fitted me well.

"For some reason I wanted to take my gloves and helmet off. The helmet and left hand glove came off all right, but my right hand glove was burned and shrivelled on to my hand which had been in the flames most of the time. I managed finally to get that glove off, but unfortunately a lot of skin came off with it, leaving my hand very raw indeed. Then I tried to right myself into the harness, but to no avail. I just couldn't do it.

"I noticed I was drifting over a small town, but I don't remember a great lot about the descent as I was in a very shocked condition, to say nothing of being badly frightened. I did notice, however, that I seemed to be heading for a ploughed field, and despite the fact that I was due to land upside down with a shock comparable to a jump from a height of nineteen feet I thought I might get away with it.

"As I came lower I could see in the corner of the field a man and his wife (at least I expected it was his wife) and I felt glad that I should be able to get such immediate help. I prepared for the landing, and protected myself as best I could in my upside-down position by winding my arms around my head and by arching my body away from the direction of travel so that I could land on my left shoulder.

"I hit the ground and opened my eyes to see that I was at least alive and that I was being dragged along the ground by the parachute. I managed to collapse it, then I sat up to release myself from the harness. When I had managed this I stood up, fully expecting the man and woman to come to help me, but they didn't. They just stood still near the house, looking at me, and probably thinking that it was just another example of RAF high spirits.

"I started to march over to them with the intention of telling them just what I thought of their behaviour, but I hadn't got very far before there was a lot of violent shouting. I looked round and saw about twenty Army types barging through the hedge with fixed bayonets, very excited soldiery telling me to so-and-so stop where I was. This annoyed me even more. I just stood and swore at them from A to Z, which convinced them that I was friendly and British. A corporal came up and asked me rather stupidly if I was hurt, which question seemed to me superfluous to say the least in view of the fact that I was limping badly, my hand was cooked, my face was red with burns, and my right trouser leg was burned off.

"However, with the corporal's help, I managed to limp down to the road by the edge of the field where one of the men had stopped a private car. In this car were two old ladies, one of whom climbed out and asked me politely whether I would prefer to sit in the front or the back. I regret to say that I told her that I didn't so-and-so mind where I so-and-so well sat. That was about all there was to it. I was driven to an Army casualty station where I was given first aid, then I was sent to the squadron's favourite hospital (the West Sussex, Brighton) where I met three of the other fellows who had been shot down in the same fight."

After being transferred to the Queen Victoria Hospital and McIndoe's surgery Lulu Lane was rested, touring aircraft factories and giving pep talks to workers whose production rate improved in the wake of visits by badly burned aircrew. Such tours, a better option than the factory work experience experiment, also benefited guinea pigs who needed to feel they were continuing to contribute to the war effort. Feeling useful and wanted was good for morale and helped to hasten a return of the confidence guinea pigs would require if like Lulu they recovered sufficiently to resume flying operations.

Roy's next posting was to the Merchant Ship Fighter Unit at Speke near Liverpool. The unit provided Hurricane aircraft and pilots for merchant ships equipped to launch them by catapult on near suicidal one-way missions in defence of convoys far out in the Atlantic. Until auxiliary aircraft carriers and longer range Coastal Command aircraft and crews became available, 'Hurricats' offered the only and slender hope of combating preying Focke Wulf Condor long-range four-engine reconnaissance bombers which were directing U-boat wolf packs towards convoys in the range gaps between British and American and Russian ports.

On May 21, 1942, Roy sailed from Iceland in convoy PQ 16 to set up and command the MSFU crews' pool and a small fighter station at Archangel to provide local cover for convoys as they approached and left port. In November he returned in convoy PQ 15 as Hurricane pilot on the freighter *Empire Moon*.

After being catapulted from a merchant ship far beyond Hurricane reach of land, Hurricat RAF and Fleet Air Arm fellow pilots could only hope to ditch or parachute and pray to be picked up. If this was an arduous and nerve testing task for a pilot who had sustained such serious injuries and burns in the Battle of Britain that at one stage McIndoe had considered amputation of his right leg, there was an arguably worse posting to follow.

Ordered to India, Roy volunteered to walk deep into Burma and operate behind the Japanese lines with the Chindits as air liaison officer to Brigadier Bernard Fergusson, the legendary Chindit leader. When Fergusson and his troops had reached their operational area they built an airstrip in the heart of Japanese-held country and a Hurricane was flown in for Lane's use.

Following a conference in India he was returning to the jungle air strip when his Hurricane developed engine trouble causing him to force-land some twenty miles east of the Chindwin river. Maps and intelligence reports on enemy positions were dropped to him but to no avail. Roy was captured by Japanese troops and never seen again. He was thought to have been beheaded. Bernard Fergusson noted: "It seemed hard that he should be missing as a result of engine failure after all his escapes in the Battle of Britain and over the Arctic convoys."

"Lulu Lane, nice chap", John Banham had said, but the Battle of Britain could have produced few 'nicer chaps' than John himself. As with Lulu, John joined the RAF before the outbreak of war on a short service commission and in 1938 had become one of the first operational pilots to fly the Spitfire when R.J. Mitchell's spanking new monoplane fighter re-equipped No 19 Squadron which had been flying Gloster Gauntlet biplanes.

Somewhat to his chagrin, John was posted in June 1940 as a flight commander to No 264 Squadron. It was a step up, but the cumbersome and ill-starred Boulton Paul Defiant which was saddled with a heavy power operated gun turret was no substitute for a Spitfire. On August 26, the day Lulu Lane was burned defending Portsmouth, John Banham had just seen a Dornier bomber "leap like a landed salmon" under fire from his turret gunner when a cannon shell from one of fifty escorting Me 109s, nosing up behind him, exploded amidships.

Fearing for his gunner John turned the blazing Defiant on its back yelling "for God's sake get out" and baled out himself, landing ten miles off Margate, the Kent resort, and swimming for nearly two hours before being picked up by a rescue launch. The gunner was never found. John Banham was promoted to squadron leader and posted to command No 229, a Hurricane squadron, arriving in time to take part in the defence of London during the early September daylight attacks on the capital.

Worn out by scrambling several times a day John was shot down again on October 15. He was badly burned, but managed to bale out of his Hurricane which crashed onto farm buildings. Following plastic surgery under McIndoe he resumed operations in 1943 as commander of No 108, a Malta-based Beaufighter night-fighter squadron which was re-equipping with Mosquitoes, moving in 1944 to command a wing in Italy.

The scene at the annual Guinea Pig Club dinner, centrepiece of the annual lost weekend, has been set previously. While its format varies little it maintains its reputation for producing new club legends and adding lustre to some of the old chestnuts. When Freeman Strickland, a cherished Australian guinea pig, attended a dinner in 1956, the maestro joshed:

> "You will remember that Strick has quite a reputation as a souvenir hunter. When he was here during the war, he managed to 'find' quite a lot of things that took his fancy – why, he even managed to remove a stag's head from the walls of this very hotel . . .
>
> "Whenever I couldn't find anything in my house, I was pretty sure that Strick had taken a fancy to it, and that the missing article was floating around Australia somewhere.
>
> "It was whispered that Strick had to pay excess freight on something like half-a-ton of stuff."

Strick, in true Australian fashion was having none of that and replied:

> "I was somewhat disgusted when I got home to find that the market value of the souvenirs was way below anything I had hoped."

After breakfast next morning, the maestro was confronted at his front door by the vast Lobster sign which had

adorned Ye Olde Felbridge Hotel, happy venue of so many
Guinea Pig Club reunions, and on the site of which guinea
pigs continue to congregate in the hotel's Jarvis group
successor. Strick, aided and abetted by his fellow Aussie,
Ken Gilkes, had succeeded in combining a demonstration
that they had not lost their touch with an inimitably
Australian expression of their gratitude to McIndoe for
hosting his traditional after-dinner party at his home, Little
Warren, until the early hours of the morning. In fairness to
Strick it should be recorded that, as with so many guinea
pigs, he matured as a sober and responsible member of his
community and among other business and public offices
became chairman of Norwich Union's boards in Australia.

Since Archie's death in 1960 and following his wife
Connie's move from Millwood Manor near East Grinstead,
Connie maintained the after-dinner tradition of entertaining guinea pigs, their wives, partners and friends. The
venue was a giant marquee, known as Connie's Big Top,
until in later years she moved her party indoors at the hotel.

Reuniting annually, the guinea pigs – so many of whom
were little more than schoolboys when an ambulance
brought them to the Sty – in their younger years threw off
in one glorious lost weekend the cares of family life,
divorce, mortgage, rent, rates and sometimes wife and
child support and rediscovered the 'wizard prang'
[wartime expression for a successful outcome to a crash]
collective humour which had sustained them at the Sty.
Some were known to have booked for dinner but failed to
have reached it after too convivial a start to the lost
weekend. They were put to bed in a ward where they were
as much if not more at home than those who had survived
until the dinner.

Inevitably, as guinea pigs have aged the lost weekend
has become less lost, but one aspect has remained constant,
the advantage of the occasion for running repairs or check
ups which led and continue to lead to more extensive work
such as in the early 1990s Bill Foxley's cornea graft, Les
Wilkins's new eyelids and Keith Base's triple heart bypass.
Known as 'Bottomly' and living and working in the West
Country, Keith built a career with Massey Ferguson the
tractor and farming company, signing letters to friends
with a drawing of a frothing tankard and serving later as a

part-time guide at Exeter Cathedral.

Les Wilkins, as with Keith, made his life in the country. After leaving the Sty he became a pig farmer, working with fingerless hands which had incisions to give some mobility and braving markets with an almost wholly reconstructed face which had taken seven years to build. In the process he met Iris Williams, the barmaid at East Grinstead's Railway Inn, a favourite guinea pig watering hole, and in 1952 they married. Les's sunny personality endeared him to all. He was the ultimate guinea pig's guinea pig. The tragedy was that he was on his second operational sortie as the rear-gunner of a Halifax bomber when in 1944 the aircraft crashed soon after take-off and he was one of only two survivors.

Tubby Taylor, a committee member of a sister club, the Goldfish Club for airmen rescued from the sea, was in every respect a great survivor. Easily distinguished by an almost congenitally cradled beer mug in the shape of a lavatory bowl and a funny hat he was hugely popular, his line of hats becoming an annual feature of the lost weekend. Beginning with a Russian *schapka* he might change to a white Pompadour wig with black bow. Over the years he sported many styles from matador's hat to gondolier's boater.

Among those who stayed the course of the 1952 dinner was Dick Atcherley, who as an air marshal was a rank senior to King Cole and, though rank was meaningless in this context, the club's most senior officer. Dick was one half of the RAF's celebrated Atcherley twins. Thanking Archie he wrote of the club: "It's a wonderful movement and I never cease to be inspired and uplifted when I depart – this time to such effect that I knocked down a wall. But it is the most eloquent tribute to your personal leadership and work."

With the passage of sixty years the lost weekend is a far tamer affair. It is doubtful that consumption by 225 guinea pigs at the 1949 dinner of 3,000 bottles of beer and 125 bottles of whisky, in addition to six dozen bottles of sherry presented by the Spanish Embassy has been exceeded – even taking into account the general substitution of wine – at one stage liberally supplied by the Australian Wine Board – as it became more available.

Although the reputation of the original Ward 3 grogging

club is by no means let down, the lost weekend gradually became more of a family affair, the very prospect of which would have horrified members in earlier times. Wives, children, and grandchildren entered the scene and the annual medical and welfare check-up presided over by Blackie and Russell for so many years extended when requested to families.

Yet the heavier load did not reduce the hearty and convivial style in which examinations were conducted and assistance offered. Thus, one finds during the boss's lifetime, a surgeon writing about Reg Hyde's son Peter, then aged two: "Dear Sir Archibald McIndoe, This little boy's mother tells me that at a guinea pig dinner you told his father that you would arrange his further treatment."

Back went the characteristic reply: "This patient's father is a guinea pig and well known to me. At the last reunion he told me a story about his child which was not nearly so clear as your very full note. . . I cannot at this moment remember what I said as the occasion was a fairly convivial one, but I have now written to the boy's father telling him that he should certainly continue under your care." And there was the cosmetic operation which the maestro was never to perform on Patsie, Sandy Sandeman-Allen's little girl and of whom Sandy wrote to Russell: "Last year Archie promised to see Patsie this year and do a cosmetic job on her ears which stick out through her hair." At East Grinstead the promise was kept.

Until his early death McIndoe, despite a heavy workload, directed and guided the Guinea Pig Club more in the style of a chief executive than a president and dotted every 'i' and crossed every 't' to make the annual reunion a resounding success. He wrote to Blackie:

> "I think the badge is pretty roughly made (former Guinea Pig badge), but what can you expect for 1s/7d? . . . Now as to the dinner menu which will be simple, homely, but good – steak, kidney and oyster pudding with Brussels sprouts and cream potatoes. This is to be carefully compounded, tasted and scrutinised by John Hunter himself. I have no further views about the guest of honour. This is very difficult. If we ask any of the big new wigs, nobody will know them, and they won't

know anybody. On the other hand there's no accounting
for the way retired RAF officers seem to sink into
senility the moment they are out of uniform . . . "

The annual dinner was formerly set in the Whitehall at East
Grinstead where the guinea pigs' great friend Bill Gardiner
helped so many of them to re-discover they could laugh
and drink, even if it necessitated drinking beer through a
rubber tube. When the beloved Whitehall, second only to
Ward 3 as shrine of guinea piggery, fell under the property
hammer Flowers, the brewers, built a new pub, The Guinea
Pig, near the hospital. Its new bricks were to mellow before
it replaced the old Whitehall with all its memories and it
also took time for the roadhouse environment of Ye Olde
Felbridge to win general acceptance as the centre of the lost
weekend.

Yet, such changes were secondary provided the Queen
Victoria Hospital and East Grinstead remained much the
same. Thus, the Sty and the attractive Sussex town remain
the true centres of pilgrimage for an annual renewal of
faith; places which, through their refusal in wartime to
accept there was nothing different about guinea pigs,
contributed as much to their recovery as Blackie, Russell,
John Hunter or the boss himself, their dedicated staff and
local supporters.

CHAPTER TEN

"Our Club . . . more exclusive than Boodle's, Buck's, White's and the Royal Yacht Squadron rolled into one."

Derek Crane was in a motor torpedo boat when it blew up at sea. One of his first impressions after the naval sick-berth attendants had delivered him from Harwich was that few inland places could be less nautical than East Grinstead. It was not simply that a sailor was a rarity among the light blue 'jobs' at the hospital. Something else was missing. Naval discipline.The boisterous irreverence which buoyed up the guinea pigs, the fearlessness of authority, the friendliness regardless of rank or rating, the calculated nonchalance which contrasted with the normal experience of senior service good order and discipline, unsettled Derek Crane.

It was a situation as distant from Derek's norm as was East Grinstead's soft Sussex scenery and sleepiness to the seaport bustle of naval bases such as Portsmouth, Devonport, or Chatham. Several months into this very different environment he remained utterly bewildered. He remembers that when he arrived at the Queen Victoria Hospital he was astonished when an RAF sergeant told the surgeon who was about to examine him: "Jerry, we've got a new patient."

Jerry was Squadron Leader Jerry Moore, a very great favourite with the guinea pigs, especially those whose hands came under his chop on the slab. Hands were Jerry Moore's speciality. Squadron Leader F.T. Moore, as the RAF medical branch knew him, was a surgeon with pilot's wings. This was an unusual combination of skills. Apart from the advantage of his being a surgeon and pilot among

aircrew patients it lent especial credence to his secondary
duty as commanding officer of RAF staff at the hospital, a
duty which to everyone's delight, he performed with a
complete lack of 'bull'. Jerry was also credited with a
somewhat wild past and stories of his exploits going the
rounds of guinea pigs in McIndoe's unconventional wards
enhanced his popularity.

Posted to the beleaguered George Cross island of Malta,
Jerry was said to have borrowed a Spitfire for an aerobatic
joy ride and to have been reprimanded after landing for
risking an aircraft which was a one-off reconnaissance
version and damaging a secret camera. Jerry was
acknowledged to be as adventurous yet never reckless in
the operating theatre where he was reputed as an
innovative surgeon. He was particularly adept at adopting
McIndoe's methods and skills and improving and adapting
instruments used in plastic surgery. Some guinea pigs were
saddened that Jerry immersed himself in private practice
after the war, lost contact, and rarely attended reunion
dinners. However, his absence in no way diminished his
guinea pig patients' gratitude and respect. Jack Toper
recalled: "Besides his ability as a surgeon the charisma he
displayed assisted many guinea pigs in their fight back to
a normal life."

Derek Crane never really understood his air force fellow
patients, but they for their part decided that this badly
burned sailor, being an odd-man-out among them, needed
an especially strong tot of guinea piggery. As a seaman he
qualified even less than Little George Hindley for
membership of the club, but like Johnny Hills and Little
George he was accepted as another exception to the aircrew
rule.

Even at this late stage sixty years on from the founding
of the club there may be ineligible former Service patients
of the Queen Victoria Hospital who, their memories stirred
by this account, will recall their long ago disappointment at
not being offered membership of the Guinea Pig Club as
was Crane and other exceptions.

However, most accepted their rejection philosophically.
One patient who was at first indignant when his
application failed, rationalised: "I was not aircrew. I was
not a burns case." He told Russell Davies: "Further, my

injuries were small with me only falling off a pushbike."
Generally, unsuccessful applicants for membership as
'exceptions' accepted they fell short of the criteria required.

Eric Pearce, though a pilot, was regarded as an exception
because he wore the 'wavy navy' rings of a Fleet Air Arm
lieutenant. He was testing a newly delivered air sea rescue
Sea Otter when the con-rod broke on take-off and he
crashed on to the shingle bank at the end of the Lee-on-
Solent, Hants, runway. Eric was pulled out of the wreckage
and a naval surgeon pinned his tongue to his cheek with a
safety pin to stop him swallowing it. Crushed by the Sea
Otter's engine which fell on top of him Eric was
"consigned to the Queen Victoria Hospital and into the
hands of Archie." When Eric recovered consciousness six
weeks later he heard church bells ringing and wondered
whether he was in heaven or on earth until somebody told
him it was VE Day.

He is one of the most regular attenders of the lost
weekends and relishes its unique status as a club
proclaimed by McIndoe as "more exclusive than Boodle's,
Buck's, White's and the Royal Yacht Squadron rolled into
one" and perpetuation of the maestro's way of doing
things. A senior officer guinea pig who, involved in a club
controversy, wrote perceptively: "My dear old Archie, we
all have our failings . . . so pardon me if I tell you that one
of yours is your habit of rushing your hurdles, of leaping
before you look, of going off half-cocked. It is a good fault
that we all accept because it does so much more good than
the general negative bluntness of most of the people of
today. It's part of you as a very successful, dynamic
character whom we all so greatly admire."

Like converts to a faith or a political party, the exceptions
strengthened their club. Derek Crane, George Hindley,
Frank Gourlay, Eric Pearce and others contributed
substantially towards this rare survival of 1940s wartime
cameraderie and purpose. Frank Gourlay was not aircrew.
In December 1943, he was a technical sergeant in No 252, a
Beaufighter squadron and en route from Cyprus to Egypt
in a Beaufighter when enemy action forced his pilot to
return to Cyprus where the aircraft hit a gun site on
landing.

Frank was able to escape quickly because he was

standing in the well behind the pilot, but realising the pilot and navigator had failed to follow him he returned to drag them out of the wreckage. Then, remembering he had been transporting the squadron's aircraft inspection documents in a steel box, he returned again and threw the box clear of the wreckage.

Just as Frank was jumping off a wing the Beaufighter exploded and he was engulfed in flames. He was repatriated and after passing through several hospitals was spotted by McIndoe during one of his trawls of RAF hospitals and transferred to the Queen Victoria Hospital where he underwent thirty-seven operations before being invalided in 1948.

For seven years Frank could not remember how he had come to be so seriously burned. Then, walking through his home village of Heacham in Norfolk he noticed a holidaymaker whom he thought he had seen before, hailed him, and discovered he was a former member of the Beaufighter squadron's equipment section in Cyprus. The visitor was astonished. He described the crash and told Frank he had thought he had died in it. In a flash, Frank's memory of that fateful day was restored.

Invariably, once wartime comrades had gone their separate ways to the various reaches of peacetime civilian life, the cameraderie and the shared anxieties of 1939-45 were overlaid by family responsibilities, fears and anxieties. Sooner or later the firmest intentions unfailingly to reunite fell victim to the demands of home life and making a living. Like old soldiers, reunions fade away.

Not so with individual rank and file members of the Guinea Pig Club who spurred by Archie, Tom Gleave, Blackie, Russell and their successors at the controls and the welfare, medical and resettlement advantages of sticking together, regarded the lost weekend as an unmissable pilgrimage. Despite diminishing numbers their continuing loyalty serves also as interest on the debt to so many others who got them on their feet and the club off the ground, not least Bernard Arch, his colleague Phil Barrowman, and Henry Standen who loyally assisted by his wife Ann, edited the club magazine for more than thirty years.

Indeed, supportive though so many wives have been, few can have matched Ann Standen's record on behalf of the club and other charitable organisations. Responsible since 1951 for so many arrangements for the lost weekends – especially catering – she remains active and will have contributed vitally to the success of the late September 2001, sixtieth anniversary reunion.

Ten years ago Ann Standen was a prime mover in helping to raise a large sum for the restoration of her church, St Swithun's in East Grinstead, and the addition of ten new stained glass windows. Each window, including one sponsored by Ann, incorporated a theme as a reminder of those who helped to pay for them. Ann's included the club's guinea pig emblem. When during the 1989 reunion guinea pigs attended their blessing Johnnie Higdon, Marchwood's Blackie, gave the address and spoke of the tablet installed as a memorial to Ann's husband, Henry.

While such sombre moments have their place in lost weekends the dinner and other events continue, in Tom Gleave's favourite phrase, to reflect the high spirits of guinea piggery. Darts matches at The Guinea Pig pub and entertainment by Max Bygraves and a host of celebrities over the years enliven the weekend.

While Archie and Connie had fostered the club's show business connections and David Lewin, the Fleet Street showbiz writer had kept them warm, individual guinea pigs sometimes gave something back by appearing on radio and television programmes themselves. Maurice Butler appeared with Esther Rantzen in a *Hearts of Gold* television programme featuring Jo Le Roy, a French man who had saved his life when on February 1943, he crashed on the beach at Cameret, south Finisterre.

Maurice, a navigator, was returning from a Bay of Biscay meteorological flight when in appalling weather his Lockheed Hudson broke cloud at 300 feet over a German convoy and his aircraft's fuel tanks were hit by flak and set on fire. He recalled:

> "We were too low to bale out so decided to make for the distant coast which was just visible. As we came nearer we saw a shelving beach and decided to make a wheels-up landing. I said 'good luck' to Sergeant Charles Glover, the pilot, and went back through some flames in the cabin to the only ditching position left to me with

my back up against the auxiliary petrol tank and sat
beside Sergeant Ernest Winfield, the rear-gunner."

On impact Maurice fractured his skull on the petrol tank
and was thrown forward and into the flames. Jo Le Roy and
another villager risked their lives to pull the four airmen –
there was also a wireless operator – out of the burning
wreckage.

After spending more than twenty months in French and
German hospitals – in one of which he encountered the
only Russian guinea pig – Maurice was much helped by an
enemy eye surgeon who somehow managed to correspond
with McIndoe for advice. In September 1944, he was
repatriated and the next month entered the Queen Victoria
Hospital.

It is a peculiar aspect of the Guinea Pig Club that,
whereas clubs tend to bring together members who are
united by interests, knowledge, pleasures, profession,
background or environment and who are ready to hoist a
black ball against those whom they dislike, McIndoe's
guinea pigs were as randomly selected as a winning line of
lottery numbers. What other club could collect such all
sorts as shop assistants like Jock Duncan and Tommy
Brandon, insurance workers like Les Syrett, bank clerks
like Pip Parratt, high ranking regular officers like Dick
Atcherley and King Cole, almost straight-from-school boys
like Owen-Smith and so on? Nothing in common here but
for being fried or mashed or frozen and generally aircrew.
Or in Les Syrett's uncompromising categorisation: "We
were all fried or mashed, fried meaning burned and
mashed covering everything else."

Pip Parratt was particularly struck by the club's all-
walks-of-life quality. He was proud of becoming a flight
lieutenant from the lower reaches of banking to which he
returned after the war. In common with Derek Crane and
Henry Standen he was another very badly hurt man who
chose to live for many years in the shadow of the Sty at East
Grinstead. Pip would have preferred to have remained in
the RAF had he been medically acceptable but accepted that
he was lucky enough to be alive after falling from 18,000
feet inside a blazing, crashing Lancaster bomber which
broke its back across a line of wagons in a Hamburg railway

yard. He maintained his connection with the RAF by serving in the Royal Observer Corps and instructing Air Training Corps cadets, to the chagrin of his first wife who as Olwen Gregory was a nurse at the hospital. She considered that Pip had done enough for his country and could spare himself long nights out in cold observation posts.

When the Germans found Pip in the wreckage of the Lancaster and the railway wagons they pulled him out into the snow, rolled him over among the railway lines and thought he was dead. Madness, the enemy said, of the British to send heavy bombers in daylight. Well, here was another Englishman who had asked for trouble. He was dead and who could say that he had not deserved it.

It was fortunate for Pip that the first Germans who found him thought no member of the crew could have survived such a crash. He heard later that, of those who had managed to bale out, the flight engineer had been shot on the end of his parachute and the rest of the crew beaten and kicked by German civilians until some members of the Luftwaffe arrived on the scene and stopped them. When McIndoe's team had repaired Flight Lieutenant Pip Parratt DFM at the Sty and equipped him with a hefty surgical boot to offset his crippling injuries, they returned him to his civilian occupation in a bank.

Pip was the most cheerful and helpful of bank tellers, but there were times, one sensed, when he wondered whether his injuries had retarded, if not killed, his chances of promotion and regretted losing the RAF career that might have been his after the war had he been considered fit enough to seek a permanent commission. Where regret or a rare touch of bitterness have been encountered among guinea pigs, such feelings were not usually born of an individual's sense of misfortune. They tended to arise from subsequent frustration. While such frustration may have been related to the origin and nature of disablement or disfigurement, it seemed to develop when life did not seem to be going too well or if a guinea pig felt cheated of opportunities and promotion at work.

Invariably in serious conversation – and this in some cases could only be achieved after gaining sufficient of a guinea pig's confidence to break through the club's banter barrier – "Did anyone tell you of the time Tubby Taylor . . .

Only 'drinking' wigs are worn at the dinner . . .What about the time Johnnie Higdon took us from Marchwood to Bournemouth and Dixie Dean brought back the keep-off-the-grass signs . . . Or the night John Hunter drank Clark Gable under the table?" – a guinea pig would reflect upon his lost opportunity of a continued career in the RAF.

Obviously the Service in peacetime could not have retained all members of aircrew who might have wished to remain in the service or to return to it once dissatisfied with civilian life. There were, however, guinea pigs who would happily have exchanged their seats on the bus to work for a bomber cabin or an airline captaincy as with Jackie Mann who flew with Middle East Airlines. This recurring dream could be unsettling.

Service as aircrew opened the prospect of new horizons to so many guinea pigs, airmen like Jock Duncan, the draper's assistant from Scotland, Sid McQuillan the Yorkshire colliery clerk, Dickie Richardson, the whistling telegraph boy who knew Worcester inside out – on his red bicycle. As Dickie said, he never dreamed of becoming one of 'those who go out to dinner' and when he did his mother who had been in domestic service told him: "Don't worry, just start with the cutlery on the outside, and eat your way inwards. Then you can't make a mistake." Comforting advice, but at first, Dickie was terrified he might get it wrong.

Understandably, this sense of 'I wonder-what-might-have-been' was stronger among those to whom their new found public respect and social elevation as aircrew commissioned officers came as a pleasant surprise and contrast, than among those who like Richard Hillary and Tom Gleave were born to it. Andre Browne, wartime flying officer and Typhoon fighter-bomber pilot, despaired that he would never rise beyond monotonous and poorly paid work as a civilian until Blackie rescued him.

Andre's resettlement was not helped by his belief that being half Belgian his broken accent was against him. There was no reason why it should have been but Andre had got it into his head that, as he said early in peacetime: "In the war a foreign accent was glamorous. Now one is just a dirty little foreigner with a bad pair of hands." The club's concern for the problems of social disability is clearly illustrated by Andre's case. He deplored the loss of confidence which had invested him when he sewed on his pilot's wings. "I am all right", he said, "until I notice that whoever I am talking to has seen my hands, and his eyes keep returning to them. Then I freeze and my foreign accent becomes all the more pronounced." Nowadays, after completing a successful and respected career as a hospital administrator Andre is a shining example of the powers of the Guinea Pig Club's unswerving efforts to help members overcome their problems.

Freddie Whitehorn, more seriously burned than Bertram Owen-Smith who was at the controls of the same bomber when the pair, making a conversion course training flight, had engine trouble and crash-landed, said: "Returning to nine to five office work after captaining a bomber seemed most unattractive." As a sergeant pilot Freddie was one of the young men who in 1938 had found adventurous release from clerking as a volunteer weekend flier. He kept a post-war interest in the RAF through his elder son and as a pilot officer in the Air Training Corps.

But there were members of the club who brooded quietly – and occasionally burst out angrily – that their injuries had held them back in civilian life, that the RAF had discovered their potential and would have provided them with a career in which their abilities would have been used. This sense of dismay was recognised by the club, particularly by Blackie and Russell, each of whom was always prepared to seek to the root of such problems and help to re-settle a guinea pig were such a course desirable. However, their problem was that not every guinea pig realised how effectively he could be counselled in such very personal circumstances and Blackie suspected that privately a number of them might be nursing an unnecessary discontent.

On the other hand it was equally understandable that a clerk who did not wish to admit to himself that he might never in any circumstances have made a manager might prefer to use his wartime injuries as an excuse for finding himself passed over.

It may seem a cruel suggestion but the saying that some men are more equal than others cannot be discounted, even when discussing such hurt men. In general, the 'playsafers' – not of course in the sense in which they fought the enemy and had perhaps been decorated – would have been happier in the armed forces which heightened their sense of personal esteem and raised their status. Equally, there were always those who, irrespective of their wounds, would have found achievement in or out of military service.

Leaving aside such considerations, it remains true that, however well, ordinarily, or badly, individual guinea pigs may have fared since they left the Sty many would have drifted or worse but for the club and re-infusions of the spirit of guinea piggery. Lecturing students during the war McIndoe said: "The suicide rate among them might be very high were it not for the fact that the right method of dealing with them is to get them out, not to treat them as people to be put behind screens." It was a measure of the success of McIndoe's common sense methods that no psychiatrist was resident at the Sty.

Bernard Arch, the RAF clerk at the Queen Victoria Hospital, who became the club's post-war honorary organising secretary, has left an unvarnished account of the traumatic experience which guinea piggery had to deal with: "The severely disfigured patient faced an abrupt change in his very personality. From knowing what he looked like and how he faced the world, he was thrown into a situation where he was not even sure of his own appearance from day to day. He expected and sought, the look of horror, or at best compassion, in the eyes of the normal person. Frequently unable to eat, or drink, or converse normally, owing to scar formation round the mouth, certain natures became morose and tended to shun all social contact. Others became unnaturally aggressive, apparently glorying in their power to shock, but suffering profound mental agonies in the darkness of the night."

Indeed, the problems of disfigurement concerned McIndoe so deeply that he persuaded Eve Gardiner, a director of cosmetics at Max Factor to advise some of his patients on the art of skilful make-up and how to apply it to help to obscure unsightly scars.Without the support of their club many of the war's most seriously injured airmen would never have left institutional life and neither the playsafers nor the commercially daring would have had the opportunity to exist or to thrive in competitive civilian life; or to keep their tail-less end up in the pensions war.

With the loss in 1960 of Archie, the boss, the maestro, guinea pigs turned more than ever to the club which year by year as the war receded gradually became not so much 'one of the curiosities of the war' but more the mother of them all, their someone-to-go-to.

CHAPTER ELEVEN

"He taught us it is great to be alive and the real joy is the gift of life regardless of handicaps." – Dr Lionel Hastings, Canadian guinea pig, on Ross Tilley.

The 1960s were watershed years in the life of the nation. Following the abandoned Suez campaign Harold Macmillan, the former Chancellor, had succeeded Anthony Eden as prime minister. Although Macmillan had made his historic 'wind of change' speech in Africa it was also a time of change at home. Guinea piggery – to recall Tom Gleave's blanket label of all matters pertaining – was swept along in the gale.

It was the beginning of times when some had it extraordinarily good, and others merely got by and the club was tireless in its efforts to prevent losers in life going on losing. In the 1960s the foundations laid twenty years earlier by Archie, Tom, Blackie and Russell stood up to the changes in society which were increasingly alien to the values of Ward 3 and the wartime 1940s. Yet, if some guinea pigs found it difficult to compete their misfortune was counter-balanced by the rise of a group of guinea pig meritocrats who were beginning to prosper and in some instances to benefit their fellow members through service to the club.

One such was James Sandeman-Allen, of whom little had been heard since Archie had repaired his shattered right arm and leg towards the end of the war. In time, though his guinea pig credentials were obscure compared with those of such better known early patients of Ward 3 as Tom Gleave, Geoffrey Page and other Battle of Britain survivors, Sandy would help to lead the club into a financially healthy new Millenium and become a force in shaping the club's future.

Sandy had returned from the Far East following the fall of Singapore as top scorer with at least seven Japanese aircraft to his name and a DFM after it. Heroism in the course of the disasters of Malaya and Singapore and subsequent defence of Java and Sumatra in February and March 1942, went largely unrecognised at the time. The exploits of Sandy and his fellow pilots were completely overshadowed by events at home. Many years were to elapse before the brief, courageous and desperate exploits of Sandy and a dwindling company of Hurricane pilots in the Far East began to receive the respect they deserved. Sandy's story exemplifies the heroism of the forgotten very few who fought above the equator against impossible odds.

In his eighties and retired from a highly successful career as a chartered accountant in the West Country Sandy, awkwardly lofty for a Hurricane cockpit, recalled how finally as the Japanese occupied Singapore he took off under fire from Japanese troops on his airfield and continued the uneven fight from the Dutch East Indies (Indonesia). Wistfully, he remembered that but for his resignation from a pre-war Sandhurst cadetship he might have been killed or taken prisoner in Malaya or Singapore as an Army officer.

Leaving Sandhurst Sandy had then been accepted for a commission in the RAFVR, but the papers were lost. Disappointed at not being called for training as a pilot he enlisted and resolutely obstructed red tape efforts to deflect him from acceptance for pilot training. In time he qualified as a sergeant pilot, was landed in West Africa from the battleship *Prince of Wales* (later to be sunk off Malaya) and presented with a Hurricane to ferry across Africa.

Setting off from Takoradi Sandy and a number of other Hurricane pilots followed a mother Blenheim light bomber to Khartoum in the Sudan. At one refuelling strip he awoke to find a giraffe inspecting his cockpit. After reaching Egypt he encountered members of No 232, his first squadron, in a bar. Learning that they were about to be ferried from Suez to the Far East in the aircraft carrier *Indomitable*, he organised a posting to rejoin them.

The prospect of a deck take-off to reinforce Singapore was daunting, but Sandy managed it safely. Operating from Kallang airfield on February 7, 1942, he jumped three Japanese Army bombers, setting one on fire and killing the gunner and damaging the other two until forced away by Zero fighters.

With the airfield under repeated attack Sandy's difficulties were compounded by the refusal of Malay and Chinese to fill in the craters, thus requiring air and groundcrew to manhandle his Hurricane over them. There were red tape frustrations too. On February 9, within days of the surrender of Singapore, he returned from combat at low level and was reprimanded for low flying during the daily siesta. On February 14 he was evacuated to Sumatra. He had been on Singapore for less than two weeks.

Hopelessly outnumbered in the final and fading resistance from Java and Sumatra, Sandy strafed landing barges and marching enemy troops. Towards the end and after destroying at least two more Zeros, Sandy's Hurricane was hit by twenty-eight cannon shells and forty-eight bullets before, wounded in the head and a leg, he landed for a cup of tea. His hand was shaking so much the cup stirred itself. Ten minutes later he scrambled again.

Shortly afterwards Sandy was allocated a seat in a Dutch KLM Lodestar airliner operating from a road at Bandoeng and flown to Perth in Australia, later returning home in charge of a party of boisterous Australian airmen. Following a short spell in the spring of 1943 as a flight sergeant with No 56, a Typhoon fighter-bomber squadron, Sandy moved to No 182 as a warrant officer. On June 30, he received the wounds which were to make him a guinea pig and eventually to leading the club as honorary treasurer and chief executive through years of devoted service which were recognised with an MBE.

Sandy had inadvertently attacked a flak train at low level when a Bofors shell exploded in the right side of the cockpit shattering his right arm and leg. Managing to fly with his left arm and setting the rudder against his useless leg Sandy turned for home. "The ends of the broken bones in my arm grinding together started to give excruciating pain and this stopped me from nodding off in the sunshine from the loss of blood. I spent the trip across the Channel trying, with great difficulty, to persuade myself that it was wiser to stay with the aeroplane and fly home than drop into the sea."

Fortunately, the Typhoon's throttle, flaps and under-carriage controls were on the left of the cockpit allowing Sandy to leave the stick momentarily. Making his approach at Tangmere he lowered the wheels, then the flaps. As he careered along the runway, a 'blood wagon' and fire tender accompanied him. Two hefty members of the squadron's groundcrew were lifting him out when his right flying boot fell off splashing blood everywhere and causing one of the airmen to pass out and fall off the wing.

Six months afterwards Sandy, though still on crutches, resumed operations with his squadron. When he was rested to qualify as an instructor the requirement to fly at higher altitudes aggravated his wounds and he was referred to McIndoe at the Queen Victoria Hospital. He was repaired and invalided from the service. Accountancy lay ahead and a busy office life in which his colleagues would have been astonished had they known that amid disaster in the Far East, Sandy had been recommended for the Conspicuous Gallantry Medal (CGM), akin almost to the VC. Such were the losses and administrative disruption that no relevant officer or papers survived to support the submission.

No such problem attended the award of the CGM to George Dove who as a flight sergeant wireless operator/air-gunner was grievously burned in a Lancaster of No 101 Squadron. George had enlisted aged eighteen after being a General Post Office telegraph messenger in Scarborough, his home town, since he was fourteen and qualified as a sergeant wireless operator/air-gunner. The next year he joined No 166, an obsolete Heyford biplane bomber squadron stationed at Leconfield in his native Yorkshire. Moving on in May 1940, to No 10 Squadron equipped with Whitleys at Dishforth, also in Yorkshire, he flew nightly sorties from nearby Leeming against barges assembling across the Channel for the invasion expected in south-east England.

On the night of October 29, 1940, George was returning from Wilhelmshaven on his thirty-first trip – one over the customary tour of bomber operations – when there was a loud bang and the skipper announced: "We've hit a balloon cable, bale out." By the time George had put on his parachute and struggled to the door there was a tremendous impact as the aircraft hit the ground and he was hurled back down the fuselage. After reaching the door again he fell into damp grass.

Nursing a broken wrist and a bleeding arm George rejoined fellow crew members who had all survived. They drank a flask of coffee until dawn when they discovered that in fact they had flown into a dead end Pennines valley hillside and the Wellington had come to rest within three feet of an eighty-foot precipice. Another three feet . . . He was awarded the DFM.

Following eighteen months rest as a gunnery instructor George had a second piece of luck. After being accidentally run over by a trolley delivering bombs to his 101 Squadron Wellington at Stradishall in Suffolk he was excused operations for the night. Within hours the Wellington was shot down into the sea and the crew perished.

On the night of February 14, 1943, when he received the burns which qualified him for membership of the Guinea Pig Club George was crewed up as a flight sergeant at Holme-on-Spalding Moor, another Yorkshire bomber base, with Sergeant Ivan Hazard as captain, three other sergeants and a pilot officer bomb-aimer.

They were leaving the target at Milan in northern Italy when they were attacked at close range by an enemy fighter and George opened fire from the mid-upper turret. His CGM citation included: "Although he was burned about the hands and face he manned his guns with grim resolution, skill and accuracy. He delivered a devastating burst at the attacker which had already been engaged and hit by the rear-gunner, and succeeded in destroying it."

But George's turret filled with smoke from four phosphorous bombs which had ignited at the rear of the bomb bay beneath his turret which became a furnace and the starboard outer engine was also on fire. The captain ordered "prepare to abandon aircraft", but hearing Airey, the rear-gunner, was badly wounded, stopped short of ordering "bale out".

George unplugged his oxygen and intercom and groped his way to the rear turret, dragged Airey out and propped him up out of the worst of the flames. He looked up the fuselage but could see nothing but fire and, realising his parachute was incinerated, resolved to share Airey's and jump with him. In this moment George was joined by the wireless operator and navigator. He grabbed a fire extinguisher and helped them fight the flames. Then, remembering the aircraft contained a huge parachute flare capable of blowing it apart, helped to manhandle it to the main door and drop it out.

At this point Hazard, diving steeply to try to put the fire out, spotted an autostrada and was thinking of crash-landing until the fire eased and he levelled out at about 800 feet. Although the three-engined bomber, devoid of hydraulics and its flaps stuck, was the wrong side of the Alps Hazard decided to make for home. Somehow, he coaxed it to 16,000 feet, crossed the Alps and with fuel streaming reached home in 10/10ths cloud with ten minutes worth of fuel left.

But where were they? According to the navigator they ought to be over the Sussex fighter field at Tangmere. There was insufficient fuel for an overshoot. Hazard SOS'd he had wounded aboard, broke cloud and there below was the illuminated Tangmere runway. The Lancaster's engines stopped dead at the hangars.

After inspecting the horrifying damage Hazard, turning his torch on George's face, gasped "Oh, my God", and helped him into an ambulance. "So", George recalled, "I went to East Grinstead where my burned face mended marvellously and I became a member of the Guinea Pig Club." He heard later that Hazard, partly re-crewed, was testing his new Lancaster when, beating up Hornsea beach, the tail wheel hit a concrete pillbox and the aircraft crashed into the cliffs killing all on board.

George returned to his squadron as a warrant officer and reckoning that after forty operations the dice would not forever fall his way, agreed to call it a day. He was commissioned and served as a gunnery instructor. Ending his war as an adjutant in Egypt he returned to the GPO, leaving to work for thirty-six years as a metal fabricator.

New Zealand-born Jim Verran was 'lost' to his fellow guinea pigs until the early 1980s when he retired to Bexhill-on-Sea in East Sussex after building a post-war career overseas in civil aviation and began to attend club events. From time to time Sandy has summoned Jim to the top table to collect a raffled bottle of whiskey amid guinea pig calls of "lucky Jim". But few of his fellow diners know how truly lucky he was to have survived not one but two horrific events which brought him to the Sty and RAF hospitals. Fortunate also in 1939 to have been commissioned after the list for New Zealanders had been closed before the authorities could reach the letter V at the tail end of the alphabet.

Deeply disappointed at being excluded during Wing Commander the Hon Ralph Cochrane's recruiting tour for the Royal New Zealand Air Force in early 1939 Jim, aged twenty-four and of Cornish and Scottish stock, took passage in the Royal Mail cargo steamer *Rimutaka*, landed with the lamb in London, obtained an Air Ministry interview and in June the next year joined No 102, a Whitley twin-engined bomber squadron stationed at Driffield in Yorkshire.

Jim had completed a tour of thirty-five operations and a spell as an instructor when in the New Year of 1943 he began a second tour with No 9, a Lancaster squadron at Waddington, Lincolnshire. On March 1 he was returning from Berlin and about to land when a Lancaster of No 57 Squadron piloted by a Canadian burst out of cloud above the airfield. Hauling back Jim thought, "That's your lot mate, you won't get out of this." The next he knew he was in a ploughed field surrounded by burning bits of his Lancaster and exploding ammunition. He learned later that the other aircraft had crashed, incinerating the crew.

Jim's jaw had been crushed when his head impacted with the control wheel, his left leg was broken and right arm paralysed and his face and head displayed the horrific results of being thrust through the Perspex canopy. He was one of four survivors of his seven-man crew. At first surgeons puzzled over earlier scars. Although they had resulted from a bomb blast crushing the back of a tunic button against his chest during a raid on Driffield airfield, Jim's story was that the neatly aligned scars each side of his body marked the passage of a bullet.

At the Queen Victoria Hospital the maestro and his team

repaired Jim's jaw and teeth and while it took time for leg, damaged lung and jaw to heal his determination to exchange surgical for bomber operations led him to the beginning of a third tour on March 5, 1944. Selected by Air Vice-Marshal Don Bennett, the Australian-born founder leader of the elite Pathfinder Force, Jim was promoted squadron leader and a flight commander in No 83, a Lancaster squadron based at Wyton, Hunts, and led by Group Captain John Searby, the celebrated Master Bomber.

On August 26, 1944, Jim took off with a full load of target markers, a 4,000 lb bomb, incendiaries and fuel to attack Koenigsberg, almost 1,000 miles away. His Lancaster was one of a total of 174 heading for the capital of East Prussia (later Kaliningrad in Lithuania). When the briefing officer told crews they were routed home over Denmark, Jim realised the course would take him over three night-fighter airfields and did not reckon much on his chances of returning to bacon and eggs and bed. Almost as if making a codicil to his will he nominated another officer as recipient of his additional eggs.

Jim was crossing Denmark – his radar unserviceable – when his Lancaster was attacked by a Me 110 from below and behind over Jutland. Verran was never sure whether the 110's Oerlikon cannon shells struck as the fighter was coming in or breaking away. What he does know is that his rear-gunner, Pilot Officer Keith Tennant, shot the 110 down before dying with the destroyed Lancaster. As for Jim, after ordering Warrant Officer Raymond Page to bale out of the burning bomber – he became a prisoner-of-war – he trimmed the aircraft to fly straight and level but found he was trapped in the bomb bay by pressure. Luckily, the Lancaster stalled, pressure reduced and, though he does not remember it, he was tossed out.

Only then as he groped in the dark for the D-ring to open his parachute did he realise that burns had closed his swollen eyelids rendering him sightless until with a superhuman effort he held his eyelids apart with his fingers, grabbed the ring and opened the canopy. As he descended he heard the Lancaster's engines above him but never heard nor saw its final dive with five crew still aboard who were probably already dead.

Jim landed perilously close to the edge of a fjord with a

sheer drop to the sea and after being cared for by a farmer was conveyed first to a local hospital by an ambulance which came under German fire. Moved to a military hospital he discovered that Major Hoefele, the 110's pilot was in a nearby bed. The hospital was short of anaesthetic and a German doctor's skin grafts were extremely painful. Jim recalls: "He used an instrument like a crochet hook which he dug into my thigh, twisted off a circle of skin and put it on my arm and legs." He found solace, however, in the tender care of a German nurse whose husband had been killed on the Russian front. As a non-smoker he gave her his daily cigarette ration to sell to other patients and buy cream cakes with the proceeds.

When Jim was fit to travel he was escorted by armed guard to the Dulag Interrogation Centre at Frankfurt-am-Main. En route on a stretcher at Hamburg railway station an air raid occurred and he was carried down into a shelter. He remembers: "There was a group of little German schoolgirls with blonde plaited hair, playing ring-a-ring-a-roses. That was bloody hard to take, realising these were the kind of people we were bombing."

During interrogation Jim was astonished to be told the Luftwaffe had recordings of his voice during bombing trials over Wainfleet Sands in Lincolnshire. Then an interrogator gave him a good laugh, confiding: "Maybe you think I know bugger nothing, but when you have been here just a while you will discover I know bugger all."

Jim was held at Stalag IXC, Moosburg near Munich, until an advancing United States tank destroyer unit freed him in April 1945. The Americans presented him with a gem of a Mercedes drophead coupe they had seized from a wealthy German family. Together with a Spitfire pilot, Bill Creed, he drove to Brussels and got a lift home in a Mosquito piloted by Flight Lieutenant Bill Kemp, a New Zealand friend. He returned later to collect the car.

Following repatriation he received further skin grafts at RAF's Cosford hospital where he was chuffed to receive a bar to an earlier DFC. In desperate need of long convalescence he spent a year on a farm at Pilsdon Manor in Dorset as the guest of the father of an aircrew friend who had been killed over Stettin. Jim spent forty-one years in senior civil aviation posts spread throughout the former colonial empire and taking in Fiji, Cyprus, and Somalia and the Cayman Islands. Since retirement he has enjoyed the cameraderie of club events.

Sid McQuillan, who is a neighbour of Jim Verran's at Bexhill-on-Sea in East Sussex, was a wages clerk in the South Yorkshire coalfield when he volunteered for aircrew in 1941. After training as a wireless operator/air-gunner he was posted to No 196, a four-engine Short Stirling bomber squadron engaged on Special Operations Executive missions to support SOE agents and the Resistance in France, towing gliders and dropping paratroops.

As with Jim he experienced an earlier mishap before burns destined him for the Queen Victoria Hospital and membership of the Guinea Pig Club. In the early hours of August 27, 1944, he was returning from dropping supplies to the French Resistance when the port outer engine failed.

His pilot continued on three engines until the dormant engine disintegrated and parts hit the inner port engine causing it to stop. Unable to maintain sufficient height to reach the home coast the pilot ditched the Stirling ten miles off Selsey Bill in Sussex. Fortunately, fishermen chanced upon the crew and Sid received a week's leave and returned to the squadron at Keevil in Wiltshire.

On February 21, 1945, Sid's Stirling, after raiding Germany, was on its final approach to a Suffolk base when it was attacked by a Ju 88 intruder night fighter whose pilot had been hoping for just such a prey. The Stirling burst into flames, the fire starting in the centre section where Sid was situated. As the pilot completed his landing Sid tried to operate a fire extinguisher but it was too hot to hold and he escaped through the aircraft's astrodome. He had spent three months in the RAF Hospital at Ely in Cambridgeshire when McIndoe arranged his removal to the Sty.

RAF service had convinced Sid that he could do better than his pre-war occupation as a wages clerk. When he returned to his job in 1948 he studied for a professional qualification. The ethos of guinea piggery at East Grinstead and McIndoe's encouragement inspired Sid's endeavours to improve his lot but at the outset he found it a struggle to clerk by day and study at night.

But Sid's effort paid off and he qualified as a chartered secretary, later being elected Fellow of the Institute.

Meanwhile, he set his sights on becoming a management accountant and, while receiving regular career promotions, eventually succeeded. He transferred from Yorkshire to the Kent coalfield where, encouraged all the way by his wife Marjorie, he became a finance/cost accountant and statistics officer. In the early 1970s Sid reckoned that a career in coal held no further opportunities and he moved to an international freight forwarding company as UK group management accountant until he retired in 1985.

"Some French, some Czechs and Poles." If the New Zealanders were omitted, presumably because they did not rhyme or scan, Blackie's inspirational verse in the Guinea Pig Club's anthem covered almost all varieties of the breed. Inevitably, the fortunes of war and the courage and bravery and occasional fool-hardiness of Czechs and Poles who fought in a spirit of 'nothing to lose' and a brooding hatred of the enemy, led to admission to the club. Some, as with Frankie Truhlar, the Czech fighter pilot who opened the celebratory bottle of sherry at the Ward 3 inaugural grogging party, were repaired and returned later to the Sty with new burns, wounds and fractures.

At times in the past sixty years it has not been easy for the club to keep in touch and, where necessary, cheer and assist its east European members whose Warsaw Pact air forces confronted Nato throughout the Cold War. Since the thaw, however, there has been easier access to those in need, enabling McIndoe's daughter Vanora Marland and Jean Ashton among others to liaise between the club and the RAF Benevolent Fund to obtain substantial assistance for them.

Since the thaw a sprinkling of Czechs and Poles who returned to their countries after the war show up from time to time at the annual lost weekend and are greeted with acclamation at the reunion dinner. Not least Alois Siska who flew with No 311, a Czech Wellington bomber squadron and who in recent years was promoted major general, the rank he is deemed to have achieved but for the long winter of Communist oppression.

Alois's story begins in 1936 when he became an airline and military pilot until Czechoslovakia was occupied and he sought anonymity in an aircraft factory and then with the Bata shoe company. After failing to steal an aircraft and fly out of the country he entered Hungary and was imprisoned.

Alois escaped from a series of prisons until, finally, he got clean away from the Citadella prison in Budapest and entered Yugoslavia moving on to Beirut in Lebanon. There he served in the French Foreign Legion until his credentials as a pilot were accepted and he was despatched to France to join a cadre of free Czech military pilots.

When France fell in the summer of 1940, Alois boarded a Danish cargo boat in Brittany and was landed in Britain where he became a bomber pilot. On December 28, 1941, he had bombed naval installations at Wilhelmshaven and was heading home when his Wellington's port engine caught fire, the engine broke loose and fell into the North Sea. Alois lost control and the bomber followed the engine into the sea. The impact knocked him out but he recovered in time to climb on to a wing only to be swept back into the icy North Sea waters. After scrambling back on to the sinking aircraft he joined four other survivors in the Wellington's dinghy. Hope blazed when a Hudson, presumably spotting their flares in the night, circled several times. It dropped a survivors' pack but the sea was too rough for the crew to reach it. Then a floating mine almost bumped into the dinghy.

On New Year's Day the second pilot and the navigator died and the wireless operator was unconscious leaving Alois and his front-gunner to discuss their fate. They decided to swallow drugs from the dinghy's medical box in expectation they would kill them. Next day, their sixth adrift, they recovered consciousness to discover the dinghy was leaking. Desperate to lighten the tiny and fragile craft Alois and his gunner tipped the body of the second pilot into the sea but were too weak to shift the navigator. Shortly afterwards they were washed up on the Dutch coast and taken prisoner.

Alois was alive but only just and doctors at the German military hospital in Amsterdam decided to amputate his legs which were suffering from frostbite and gangrene. But, as he reached the operating table, Alois had a heart attack and the operation was abandoned. Alois's legs responded in some measure to treatment and he was held in a number of prisoner-of-war camps until in July 1944, the Gestapo removed him to Prague where he was charged with high treason and espionage against Germany. Afterwards, he was lodged in Colditz to await trial.

But the Gestapo was so heavily committed with investigations and arrests arising from the failed attempted bomb assassination of Hitler that he was left at Colditz until April 15, 1945. The day before Allied troops entered the castle, he was moved to another camp where, seizing rifles from the guardroom, he took charge shortly before VE Day. As American tanks approached Alois grabbed a white sheet and staggered up to them on crutches. The RAF landed him at Manston in Kent on May 15. It was his thirty-first birthday. He underwent two years of surgery at the Queen Victoria Hospital before returning to Czechoslovakia.

Among French aircrew whose status as guinea pigs justified their inclusion in Blackie's anthem Commandant Jacques Henri Schloesing, who was credited with eighteen enemy aircraft destroyed and whose chestful of decorations included the George Cross, fought on after the fall of France in 1940 until he was shot down over France in February 1942, and badly burned. Resistance members sheltered and nursed him until he was fit enough to be smuggled back to Britain where he was treated at the Queen Victoria Hospital.

Impatient to return to the Alsace Squadron, he defied medical advice and rejoined the war in the summer of 1944 and was shot down over Normandy on August 26, the day Paris was liberated and where a street has since been named in his memory. Later the commandant was similarly honoured by the small Normandy town of Beauvoir-en-Lyon. In the course of a street naming ceremony in 1984 an RAF Spitfire and a pair of Alsace Squadron aircraft flew over his tomb in salute to his memory.

Over the years a strong bond has remained between the club and members who returned after the war to Britain's former dominions and liberated countries in western Europe, while in more recent times links have been renewed with airmen such as Siska – the last surviving Czech guinea pig – who escaped from eastern Europe and continued the fight.

In 2000, thanks to the generosity of Jan Horal, another Czech who flew with the RAF but was not a guinea pig and who had attended the previous year's reunion dinner, a party of guinea pigs and their wives or widows spent a week in the Czech Republic. Centred on Jan's own hotels in Prague and Cesky Krumlov the visit was orchestrated by his wife, Phyllis, and on behalf of the guinea pigs by the irrepressible Jack Perry. Greatly impressed by the club's long and mutually beneficial relationship with the RAF Benevolent Fund Jan also invited Air Chief Marshal Sir David Cousins whom he had met at the dinner.

Amid the lunches, dinners and parties – in the tradition of Ward 3 and guinea piggery – there were suitable occasions for remembrance and reflection. Jan's guests were particularly moved when they were shown a film about the fate of Czech airmen who returned to Czechslovakia and suffered under the Communist regime; a sobering reminder of how some were imprisoned and others sent to labour in the mines.

EPILOGUE

"These people were damaged, their souls and their spirits."
– Jane McDonough from Glasgow who married the
Canadian guinea pig Ed Smith.

Sixty years on from the founding grogging party today's patients and visitors at the Queen Victoria Hospital are initially unaware of the hospital's role when Britain and her empire were fighting to rid Europe of German oppression and defeat the Japanese aggressor in the Far East. But it is not long before the sick and their relatives and friends begin to sense that something quite unusual took place in a hospital where the name McIndoe remains ubiquitous.

For instance, visitors may discover that the canteen where they are taking lunch or tea was formerly the hutted Ward 3 and that the neat little garden nearby is dedicated to the Guinea Pig Club; close inspection being rewarded with some excellent topiary in the shapes of a Spitfire and a guinea pig.

Those who wish to learn more can visit the museum which contains a superb collection of guinea pig memorabilia, mementos and artifacts relating to the wartime work of McIndoe and his team. The museum contains a library and chairs and tables for visitors wishing to dip into or research among the library's comprehensive collection of books by and about guinea pigs and their club. A full set of *Guinea Pig*, the club magazine, is available. There is assistance too from Bob Marchant, a retired former member of the RAF medical branch and Queen Victoria Hospital staff whose knowledge of the subject is encyclopaedic.

The museum was the inspiration of John Bennett and

Tom Cochrane, senior consultant plastic surgeons who conceived it twenty-five years ago. Tom's collection of photographs of former consultants is ranged either side of an enlarged and centrepiece portrait of Sir Archibald McIndoe.

Each surgeon in his day was closely associated with the Guinea Pig Club, particularly Tom who, following twenty-seven years service, retired from the Queen Victoria Hospital in 1992. Tom, who served formerly in the RAF medical branch, enjoys a natural and warm empathy with the guinea pigs and as the club's honorary plastic surgeon maintains McIndoe's tradition of a 'garage hand ever ready for running repairs'. Fortuitously, Bob Marchant combines his museum activities with duties as barman in the hospital surgeons'mess. So he is on hand when the surgeons or their visitors wish to refer to him on specific points of hospital or guinea pig history.

Whereas the museum records and explains so much of the hospital's past, new buildings and departments created in McIndoe's name outwardly represent his legacy to contemporary burns treatment and forward research. Even as he fostered the rehabilitation and resettlement of his guinea pigs in the early post-war years, McIndoe was seeking scientific advances which in time would greatly improve surgical and treatment techniques in various areas of plastic surgery. McIndoe determined to establish a research centre attached to the hospital. His initial aim was to drive forward exploration of how to treat burns injuries and reconstruct missing tissue.

The Guinea Pig Club's wealthy supporters living in the neighbourhood of East Grinstead rallied round and McIndoe's close friends Neville and Elaine Blond were immediately enthusiastic and supportive. Their substantial financial contribution helped to build the Blond McIndoe Centre, enabling the Leverhulme Trust to launch its first research project. Another early supporter was Sir Max, later Lord Rayne. Since the 1960s the list of donors has grown appreciably. In 2000, for instance, Merrill Lynch Investments Managers through the efforts of Sarah Hanna raised upwards of £30,000. Sadly, Sir Archibald died in 1960 before research work began but more than forty years on, the Centre perpetuates his memory and takes forward his pioneering advances in wound healing, skin culture and other surgical developments. The maestro is also remembered on the English Heritage blue plaque which Connie unveiled outside their former London home in Chelsea.

In these early years of the new Millenium Blond McIndoe remains indebted to its guinea pig origins and the maestro. If the Centre's direction and research is undertaken by dedicated successors to McIndoe and his team members its trustees will provide links between its current achievements and its past. More than forty years on from her husband's death Connie McIndoe, Sam Gallop who suffered third degree burns and lost his legs as a pilot and the Blonds' son and daughter, Peter Blond and Dame Simone Prendergast keep the Centre's plastic and reconstructive surgery on course in the McIndoe tradition. They also help to guide the Centre's use of substantial sums allocated regularly by the McIndoe Guinea Pig Memorial Trust, a capital trust established recently to employ some of the Guinea Pig Club's accumulated funds. By 2001 a sum of £400,000 had been transferred. In the year 1998-1999 the Centre moved part of its research to the Royal Free Hospital's medical school within the University College of London.

Here, as visiting guinea pigs Jack Toper, Jack Allaway and Bill Foxley learned, research undertaken in the Blond McIndoe laboratories has concentrated on the next surgical revolution. Professor Colin Green, Blond McIndoe director for ten years until 2000 when he handed over to Dr Giorgio Terenghi, his deputy director, outlined this as tissue engineering and stem cell transplantation.

Inevitably, not every guinea pig approves of such a major dispersal of club funds which have been diligently increased and protected over the years under the stewardship of Sandy Sandeman-Allen, helped by Cazenoves in the City and other investment advisers. Some members, possibly fearing problems as they age, favour a per head distribution to survivors or retention of capital to assist their welfare or that of their widows in their remaining years. But the majority, as indicated at recent annual general meetings, accept Sandy's recommended policy and approve retention of just £300,000 of club funds for the benefit of members as needs arise.

Moreover, members are aware that come what may the RAF Benevolent Fund is ever ready to assist irrespective of a sum of £50,000 placed with it in a special account by the Guinea Pig Club and declared for the exclusive assistance of guinea pigs whose cases are submitted by Vanora Marland, McIndoe's daughter, and other members of the Fund-Club liaison committee.

After making the above series of arrangements Sandy Sandeman-Allen, Jack Allaway and Jack Toper, the Guinea Pig Club's trustees and their fellow committee members Ann Standen, Jean Ashton and Bill Simpson have assured as best they can the future wellbeing of their club and the welfare of their fellow members.

SELECTIVE BIBLIOGRAPHY

Dickson, Lovat *Richard Hillary* (Macmillan, 1950)

Donahue, Arthur Gerald *Tally Ho (Yankee in a Spitfire)* (Macmillan, 1941)

Donovan, Rita *As for the Canadians* (Buschek Books, 2000)

Faulks, Sebastian *The Fatal Englishmen* (Hutchinson, 1996)

Formanek, Vitek *Stories of Brave Guinea Pigs* (J&KH Publishing, 1998)

Gleave, Tom *I had a Row with a German* (Pan Books, 1956)

Hillary, Richard *The Last Enemy* (Macmillan, 1942)

Hodgkinson, Colin *Best Foot Forward* (Corgi Books, 1978)

Kelly, Terence *Hurricane & Spitfire Pilots at War* (Arrow, 1988)

McLeave, Hugh *McIndoe Plastic Surgeon* (Frederick Muller Ltd, 1961)

Mosley, Leonard *Faces from the Fire* (Weidenfeld & Nicholson, 1962)

Page, Geoffrey *Shot Down in Flames* (Grub Street, 1999)

Pape, Richard *Boldness be my Friend* (Granada Publishing, 1984)

Ross, David *Richard Hillary* (Grub Street, 2000)

Simpson, William *I Burned my Fingers* (Putnam Books, 1955)

Simpson, William *One of our Pilots is Safe* (Hamish Hamilton, 1942)

Simpson, William *The Way of Recovery* (Hamish Hamilton, 1944)

Williams, Peter and Ted Harrison *McIndoe's Army* (Pelham Books, 1979)

Willis, John *Churchill's Few* (Michael Joseph Ltd, 1985)

THE GUINEA PIGS

J. Adamczyk
J. G. Adams
R. R. Adams
R. Adcock
H. Aldridge
J. A. Allard
J. Allaway
G. W. Allen
T. Allen
K. Allison
H. Anderson
I. Anderson
J. Anderson
J. A. Anderson
L. Anderson
J. R. Andrew
W. G. Anglin
J. P. Angold
R. I. Armstrong
J. D. Ashton
D. J. Aslin
R. L. R. Atcherley
M. R. Atherton
J. C. Atkinson
D. Bacon
R. Bagard
J. H. Bain
A. R. Ball
R. J. Ball
F. A. Ballentyne
A. J. Banham
V. Banks
W. D. Barber
J. S. Barker
A. A. Barrow

P. Barry
K. M. Base
G. E. Beauchamp
W. Begbie
J. Benbow
G. C. Bennett
G. H. Bennions
G. H. Bernier
N. E. Berrington-Pickett
L. E. Berryman
M. Biddle
J. Biel
F. Bielawski
H. Bird-Wilson
J. B. W. Birks
M. Bobitko
C. Boissonas
D. E. B. Bond
H. Van Dyke Bonney
W. J. Bourn
A. C. Bowes
W. M. Bowyer
C. I. L. Boyd
G. P. Bradley
P. F. Branch
T. W. Brandon
K. Branston
C. Briggs
E. Bristow
R. Broadbent
E. Bronski
P. W. S. Brooke
R. H. Brooke
N. Brooks
J. Broughton

T. Brown
A. H. R. Browne
K. Browne
T. Browne
E. Brunskill
J. D. Bubb
J. W. Buckee
F. G. Buckle
H. W. Buckman
V. G. Bull
E. G. Buller
F. Bullock
G. Burrell
W. G. Burton
G. Butcher
J. C. Butler
M. W. Buttler
L. Caddell
B. S. Cadman
E. A. Cain
L. Cameron
B. Campbell
C. Campbell
K. Cap
J. Capka
J. Carlier
E. L. Carlsen
R. Carnall
E. M. Cartwright
L. P. Catellier
E. Cecille
E. Chapman
M. Charbonneau
R. W. H. Charles
C. Chater

L. E. Chiswell
R. G. Chitham
G. B. Clarke
J. R. Clarke
R. Clarkson
R. Cleland
J. Clifford
J. Colbert
A. T. Cole
J. Cole
L. P. H. Cole
G. Collier
R. Collin
R. Colyar
J. Condon
A. Cooke
C. Cooper
K. G. Cooper
W. Cooper
M. Coote
P. Coppock
A. Corpe
L. R. Corrigan
W. Cowham
J. W. Craig
S. Crampton
D. Crane
D. Crauford
H. R. Crombie
W. G. J. Cruickshank
J. Cummins
W. Cunningham
H. Curwain
G. Dakin
R. W. Dalkin
E. D. Dash
C. E. Davidson
K. Davidson
F. S. Davies
K. Davies
J. Davis
P. Davoud
E. J. Davy

F. G. Davy
R. L. F. Day
F. J. Dean
L. Dean
K. B. L. Debenham
G. De Bruyn
H. J. Dee
E. J. De Lyon
A. Deniall
T. Derenzy
M. Dermerdash
F. Devers
W. Dewar
W. A. Douglas
G. Dove
O. Dove
E. A. Doyle
W. Doyle
A. S. Dredge
G. Dufort
G. Duncan
J. W. Duncan
R. D. Dunscombe
P. Edmond
G. Edmonds
W. Edmonston
G. D. Edwards
H. Edwards
A. Elkes
P. R. Ellis
N. Erakdogan
H. Ernst
J. Evans
J. Everett
H. Fairclough
F. Falkiner
G. R. Fawcett
E. Ferguson
J. Ferguson
G. Figuiere
S. G. Finnemore
K. Fisher
P. H. Fitzgerald

J. Fleming
G. Forbes
M. E. Forster
G. L. Fowler
R. P. Fowler
W. J. Foxley
R. A. Fraser
R. Fraser
R. G. Fredericks
D. Freehorn
H. M. Friend
S. R. Gallop
R. Gambier-Parry
A. H. Gambling
T. A. Garne
R. Garvin
R. Gauvin
V. P. Gerald
F. G. Gibbs
C. Gilkes
J. Gillies
J. Gingles
G. B. Giradet
S. Given
T. P. Gleave
J. Glebocki
D. R. Glossop
N. W. Glover
W. Golding
C. E. Goodman
L. A. Goodson
J. F. Gourlay
R. Graham
A. Graveley
H. T. Green
J. Grill
J. Grudzien
J. N. Gunnis
E. Gwardiak
J. Haddock
L. Haines
D. Hall
N. D. Hallifax

K. Hall
F. Hanton
J. Harding
C. Harper
J. Harrington
W. W. Harris
L. R. W. Harrison
K. Harrop
P. R. Hart
D. Harvey
F. R. Haslam
L. E. Hastings
A. J. Hawksworth
W. Heine
D. A. Helsby
A. J. Henderson
A. C. Henry
J. Heslop
G. Hewison
R. J. Hewitt
W. R. Hibbert
C. Hicks
D. Hicks
J. Hicks
W. J. Higgins
E. Hiley
J. P. Hill
N. Hill
W. Hill
R. Hillary
A. J. Hills
G. J. Hindley
C. Hitchcock
V. R. Hobbs
W. W. Hocken
C. G. S. Hodgkinson
R. Holdsworth
R. H. Holland
N. P. C. Holmes
N. Holmes
W. Holmes
J. Hood
J. Hooper

R. Houston
F. Hubbard
J. Hughes
J. D. E. Hughes
W. S. Humphreys
D. W. Hunt
C. O. Hunter
C. A. L. Hurry
G. W. Hutchinson
W. J. Hutchinson
R. H. J. Hyde
K. Intepe
N. L. Ireland
G. E. Jackson
J. W. F. Jacob
G. T. Jarman
J. Jarman
C. R. Jenkins
G. R. Johnston
B. Jones
I. M. Jones
I. W. Jones
J. S. Jones
O. Jones
F. Keene
J. Keep
J. K. Kelly
J. H. F. Kemp
J. Kerr
F. P. King
B. Kingcome
J. Kirby
J. J. Knott
W. Knowles
W. P. Korwell
J. Koukal
E. Krasnodebski
P. S. Kyd
E. LaCasse
N. Lambell
E. G. Lancaster
D. Lanctot
A. Lander

R. Lane
W. Lane
N. C. Langham-Hobart
A. Langland
S. Langley
G. Lawson
G. T. Lea
R. G. F. Lee
S. M. Lee
T. M. Lee
A. Leitch
J. Lestanges
R. Leupp
E. J. Lever
J. Levi
B. Levin
W. H. Liddiard
E. S. Lightley
M. Lipsett
R. T. Lloyd
E. S. Lock
B. Loneon
S. Loosley
A. J. Lord
R. C. Lord
G. J. Lowe
J. Lowe
S. Lugg
D. M. Lunney
L. Lymburner
J. McBride
S. MacCormac
A. C. H. Maclean
J. F. MacPhail
W. J. MacPherson
O. J. McCabe
R. C. McCallum
A. McConnell
G. McCully
T. McGovan
R. A. McGowan
B. McHolm
I. C. S. McIvor

T. D. McKeown
J. McLaughlin
C. MacLean
C. A. McLeod
D. McNally
D. C. McNeill
S. McQuillan
D. McTavish
R. Major
J. Mann
J. Marceau
J. Marcotte
C. Marjoram
J. Marshall
D. D. Martin
J. Martin
S. Martin
W. Martin
W. Martin
D. C. Marygold
R. M. Mathieson
J. Mathis
J. W. Maxwell
J. May
L. Melling
J. C. Melvill
W. R. Methven
J. Miles
N. E. Miles
W. H. Mills
B. Mitchell
S. R. Molivadas
E. G. S. Monk
J. F. Montgomery
M. Montpetit
O. G. Moore
F. S. Moores
J. Mordue
A. Morgan
I. C. A. Morris
H. J. Morson
M. H. Mounsdon
G. D. Mufford

J. G. E. Munt
G. D. I. Neale
R. G. Nelson
A. Nesbitt
B. P. Nettleton
N. Newman
W. Newson
T. Nichols
N. Nisbet
J. Nivison
B. R. Noble
G. Noble
W. L. Noble
R. Noon-Ward
C. T. Norman
S. A. Noyes
J. B. O'Brien
D. O'Connell
K. O'Connor
H. Ogden
T. O'Halloran
E. Orchel
G. Orman
D. O'Sullivan
F. Overeijnder
E. Owen
A. G. Page
R. B. Pape
H. E. Parratt
A. Paszkowski
R. H. Payne
T. J. Peach
E. G. Pearce
G. H. Pearce
R. E. Pearce
A. Pearson
H. Peel
F. Penman
P. Pereuse
E. J. Perry
D. Petit
H. Phillips
L. Phillips

S. A. Piercy
D. Pike
J. Pitts
M. A. Platsko
T. A. Podbereski
E. Poole
J. Poole
K. L. Porter
R. F. Pretty
D. Price
B. Propas
A. Proudlove
D. M. Pryor
F. J. Quigley
I. Quilter
G. H. Raby
R. Ralston
H. J. Randall
R. F. G. Raphael
V. Rasumov
J. Redekopp
J. Reece
C. G. Reynolds
G. Reynolds
J. Reynolds
S. Reynolds
C. Rhodes
D. B. Richardson
W. Richardson
J. Rickard
B. Ridding
F. T. Rix
E. D. Roberts
E. J. Robbins
J. L. Roberson
R. Roberts
T. J. Roberts
A. B. Robertson
J. H. Rogers
S. Round
A. Rowley
A. Royds
J. H. Russell

K. Russell
J. St. John
J. F. M. Sampson
J. A. Sandeman-Allen
A. C. Saunders
R. T. Saunders
J. H. Schloesing
T. J. Scoffield
E. E. Scott
J. E. Scott
G. R. Scott-Farnie
D. R. Scrivens
R. Shallis
A. Shankland
W. Shankland
W. Simms
D. W. Simpson
J. H. Simpson
W. Simpson
J. A. Sims
A. Siska
L. Skoczylas
B. O. Smith
D. B. Smith
J. Smith
J. C. Smith
P. C. Smith
P. S. S. Smith
R. J. Smith
T. A. Smith
T. C. F. Smith
T. G. Smith
W. E. Smith
R. Smith-Barry
K. C. Smyth
A. B. Snelling
K. Snyder
L. J. Somers
J. Southwell
G. L. Spackman
W. R. Speedie
B. Spooner
W. H. C. Spooner

J. W. Squier
J. Stafford
H. H. Standen
E. Stangryciuk
  (E. Black)
W. M. Stanley
H. Stannus
A. Stansberg
D. Stephen
D. W. R. Stewart
H. J. Stickings
P. Stoker
C. Stone
F. Strickland
G. A. Stroud
G. Struthers
D. Stults
J. B. Sullivan
A. K. Summerson
P. W. Sutton
F. Swain
L. Syrett
M. Szafranski
R. Tait
W. Tanner
R. Tarling
R. Tatajczak
H. Taubman
B. Taylor
D. Taylor
E. A. Taylor
G. F. Taylor
J. E. Taylor
D. F. Tebbit
A. G. Thomas
J. Thomas
D. L. Thompson
J. J. Thompson
J. M. V. Thompson
G. W. Tiplady
A. H. Tollemache
J. J. Toper
J. Tosh

W. Towers-Perkins
K. N. Townsend
J. K. Trask
J. R. Treagust
L. Tremblay
F. Truhlar
K. S. Tugwell
L. Tully
R. Turnbull
G. Turner
J. Varty
J. Verran
D. L. Vince
E. Vincent
R. Vivian
T. E. Voges
L. Wainwright
A. E. Wakley
C. Walker
T. C. Walshe
K. C. Warburton
C. G. A. Ward
H. C. Ward
W. C. Warman
P. Warren
C. R. Warwick
J. T. Waterson
C. Watkins
F. Watkins
H. Watkins
P. J. Weber
F. Webster
P. C. Weeks
P. H. V. Wells
J. Welsh
J. Weston
F. V. Whale
B. G. Whalley
R. Wham
J. White
N. White
R. F. Whitehorn
M. W. E. Wild

C. Wilkes	G. Wilson	F. G. Woollard
L. R. Wilkins	M. Wilton	R. Worn
G. Wilkinson	J. J. Wishart	C. M. Wright
H. Williams	I. A. Wood	D. Wright
S. R. Williams	H. W. Woodward	J. E. F. Wright
T. Williams	P. A. S. Woodwark	R. C. Wright
T. W. Williams	G. E. Wooley	
V. Willie	A. Woolf	

Note: This list contains the names of all recorded Guinea Pigs.

INDEX